THE RAFTSMEN

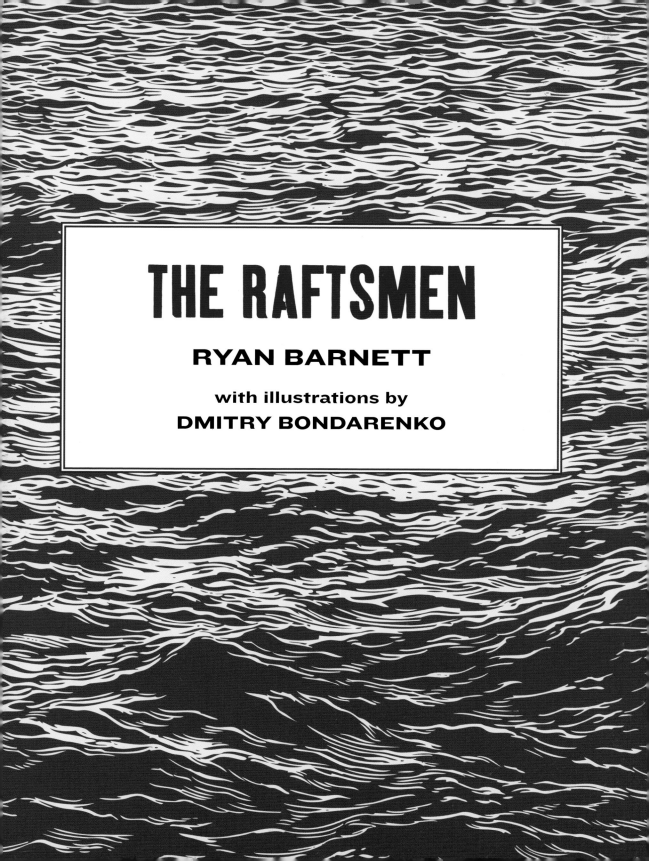

THE RAFTSMEN

RYAN BARNETT

with illustrations by
DMITRY BONDARENKO

A Firefly Book

Published by Firefly Books Ltd. 2017

First printing

Publisher Cataloging-in-Publication Data (U.S.)

Names: Barnett, Ryan M., 1982-, author. | Bondarenko, Dmitry, illustrator.

Title: The Raftsmen / Ryan Barnett ; with illustrations by Dmitry Bondarenko.

Description: Richmond Hill, Ontario, Canada : Firefly Books, 2017. | Summary: "A dramatic retelling of four adventurers who crossed the North Atlantic on a raft, featuring archival photography … contemporary interviews and original illustrations" – Provided by publisher.

Identifiers: ISBN 978-1-77085-978-4 (hardcover)

Subjects: LCSH: Atlantic Ocean. | Transatlantic voyages. | L'Egare II (Raft). | Canada – History – 1945-.

Classification: LCC G530.L44B376 |DDC 910.45 – dc23

Library and Archives Canada Cataloguing in Publication

A CIP record for this title is available from Library and Archives Canada

Published in the United States by
Firefly Books (U.S.) Inc.
P.O. Box 1338, Ellicott Station
Buffalo, New York 14205

Published in Canada by
Firefly Books Ltd.
50 Staples Avenue, Unit 1
Richmond Hill, Ontario L4B 0A7

Cover and interior design: Marijke Friesen

Printed in China

Canada We acknowledge the financial support of the Government of Canada.

For Sonia and Esmé, who keep me afloat every day.

For Pop, the prolific writer in the family.

And for Mom, who will never read this book
but is never far from my mind.

— R. B.

TABLE OF CONTENTS

FOREWORD

ILLUSTRATED STORIES have long told tales of heroes performing great acts of "derring-do," so it is entirely appropriate that this story of four men attempting to cross one of the world's most dangerous oceans on a structure made entirely of cedar logs tied with rope receives the same treatment. In *The Raftsmen*, Ryan Barnett masterfully mines content from original interviews, archival documents, news stories, memoirs, journals and logs — as well as a treasure trove of pictures from the voyage — to help tell this fascinating story, which is given further depth and character through the comic illustrations of Dmitry Bondarenko.

The Raftsmen takes readers into the nearly forgotten world of Henri Beaudout and the teams he put together to cross the frigid and brutal North Atlantic via raft. The mission certainly tested the young men's mettle, but its main intent was to prove Beaudout's theory that prevailing winds and ocean currents would take an unpowered craft to Europe on the North Atlantic by way of the Gulf Stream — provided it could stay afloat, of course.

I was born the year Beaudout made his first attempt, in 1955, and just learning to walk when he succeeded on his second, in 1956. Yet I heard nothing about these daring voyages until I was in my mid-fifties.

By then, I was a well-seasoned Canadian journalist who thought I'd heard it all. How could I not have known about these two teams of Montreal residents who had placed nothing but a raft between themselves and the powerful North Atlantic? In Norway, a raft called the *Kon-Tiki* had crossed the more languid Pacific and is celebrated to this day with its own museum. Beaudout named both his rafts *L'Égaré*, meaning "the lost one" — an apt choice in retrospect as they have achieved little recognition up to now.

I was first introduced to Beaudout's adventures by a retired sea captain in St. John's, Newfoundland, named Caleb Kean. Captain Kean had encountered the second raft on the Grand Banks in 1956, and, in 2012, he showed me memorabilia of the journey.

"I wonder if any of them is still alive?" he asked. I decided to find out.

By a twist of fate, Beaudout had been invited out of obscurity just a week earlier to speak to a group of sailing enthusiasts in Quebec City. I found notice of his talk online. When I reached him by telephone at his home in Montreal, he told me he was the only one of the raftsmen still alive, and he asked if I wanted to read his recently published memoir, *Les Égarés*.

When the book arrived, the package also included a DVD of film footage shot by *L'égaré* crewmate Gaston Vanackere. I was astounded to see dramatic scenes of Captain Kean, then 29, rowing a boat toward the raft, preparing to evacuate the cook, Jose Martinez, who had lost heart for the expedition after becoming terribly seasick. When I showed the 60-year-old footage to Kean, he should have been surprised to see it, but instead, he kept his eyes glued to the sea. "There was some swell on," he commented.

Indeed there was, and many times even bigger swells threatened to swamp the raft and its crew.

RoseMarie Comeau-Maher, who had been Henri's translator in Nova Scotia when the raft was built and who'd had the honour of launching it with an empty bottle of champagne, was startled to hear Beaudout's voice when my CBC radio documentary *Atlantic Kon-Tiki* was broadcast. The rekindling of friendship that ensued has meant a great deal to these two comrades in adventure. When *Atlantic Kon-Tiki* won a silver New York Festivals International Radio Program award in 2014, Henri and I travelled by train from Montreal to attend the gala. Now he calls me "ma journaliste." More recently, I attended the opening of the Musée maritime du Québec's permanent exhibit of the historic journey, later joining Henri and his daughter Chantal for supper on a terrace overlooking the St. Lawrence River — a spot Henri recalled floating past on his first voyage in 1955.

We are so lucky to have Beaudout, Kean and Comeau-Maher around in 2017 to remind us that dreams can become reality when you surround yourself with fellow dreamers. Ryan Barnett and I have certainly been swept up in the current of this story, and we hope this unique retelling will carry you along with us.

— Marie Wadden, 2017

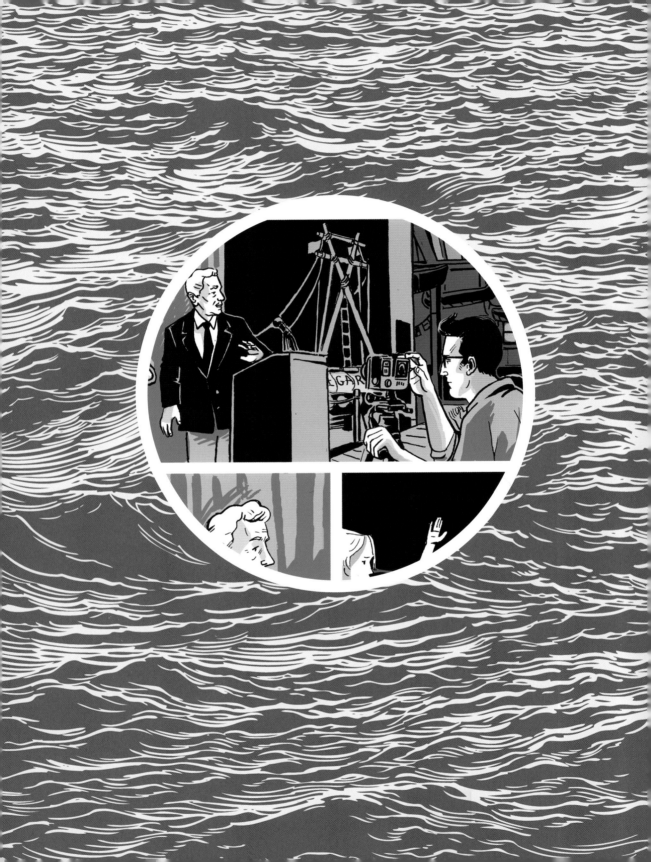

iNTRODUCTiON

IN THE SUMMER of 2012 — on hiatus from the third-rate Canadian television series I was working on at the time — I drove the seven-and-a-half-hour trip from Toronto to the tiny village of Neuville, Quebec, to hear Henri Beaudout speak about his experiences aboard *L'Égaré II*, the raft he built for his second oceanic expedition. I did this for a few reasons, but to get you into the pages of this book as quickly as possible, I'll give the condensed version that I have told countless times to the curious and uninitiated over the past five years.

In 1956, three men and two kittens crossed the Atlantic Ocean on a primitive log raft that was little more than nine telephone poles lashed together with a mile of rope. The story of *L'Égaré II* has all the hallmarks of a great pulp adventure: an oceanic expedition, a shipwreck, a daring mid-sea rescue, a perilous battle with sharks and a quixotic captain at the centre of the action. Captain Henri Beaudout was the architect of the expedition, and now, at 90 years old, he is also the sole remaining member of its crew.

At the time I first heard Henri's story, I was entering the second year of a two-year master's program in film studies. Up to that point, I had spent much of my studies focusing on ethnographic filmmaking and travelogues. I wrote about films like *La Soufrière* (1977, Werner

Herzog), *Life Without Death* (2000, Frank Cole) and *Kon-Tiki* (1950, Thor Heyerdahl). I was immediately attracted to this little raft and its journey across the North Atlantic due to its potential as a subject for a documentary film. I had been looking for something to pitch as a major research project for my master's thesis for some time, and this story — this largely forgotten moment of romantic inspiration during an era of adventure characterized by the likes of Thor Heyerdahl, Sir Edmund Hillary and Yuri Gagarin — sparked my imagination.

While doing some cursory Internet research on the voyage, I came across an announcement that Henri Beaudout was scheduled to speak at a conference in Neuville during my upcoming time off. So I made the drive to the small Quebec village, arriving just in time for his talk. I stood in the back of a packed room on the second floor of their city hall, waiting for the end of the presentation so I could introduce myself to Henri and ask him to make a film with me.

While I waited, I also saw what was left of the original raft: a one-metre (three-foot) long segment from one of the logs and a length of manila rope encrusted in sea salt. I watched with the crowd as Remi Morissette, then-president of the Neuville Historical Society, unveiled these recently discovered remnants to Henri for the first time. In that moment, from the back of the room, I swear I registered a look of displeasure on Henri Beaudout's face. Here he was, facing Morissette's enthusiasm for this find, and to my eye, he could barely disguise his indifference to the artifacts in front of him. It was a funny scene to observe, and I later discovered it was emblematic of Henri's personality. His feelings toward *L'Égaré II* and its ending are complicated — he wasn't just some elderly man trading on his past laurels for a quick pat on the back — he still had unfinished business with his raft.

The documentary film that shares its name with this book is a breezy 16 minutes long and took four years to make. For reasons both inside and outside my control, production was protracted, and the original concept had to be adjusted to fit a shorter format. As a result of boiling four years of research and filming into a 16-minute runtime, a lot of great stuff went by the wayside. When I was offered the opportunity to make a book on the subject, I was excited to explore and use the elements I hadn't been able to include in the film. That meant going back over the countless interviews I'd done to mine more content. These interviews support much of the structure of the story presented here.

RoseMarie Comeau-Maher and Cyril Henneberry are two figures I hadn't been able to feature in the film, but my interviews with them enrich so much of the early chapters of this book. RoseMarie, in particular, had a unique and privileged relationship with *L'Égaré II* and its crew, and I am both pleased and proud to include her story in the official record of the journey.

I also uncovered some new material in the process of researching for this book, for example, the advertisement from *Le Petit Journal* (see page 43) that Henri had used to find his crew for his 1955 voyage. I had been unsuccessful back in 2013 when I first searched for it. I had all but given up, until one night, I decided to take another run at the Grande Bibliothèque's online archive. I went through issue after issue from 1954 onward, not knowing exactly what I was looking for. Finally, I spotted a small picture of Henri with a cocky, daring look in his eye. It was on page 34 of the April 3, 1955, issue. I hadn't found it in 2013 because I never imagined Henri would still have been looking for his crew so close to the anticipated departure date.

Another monumental find for me was Mireille Modena, daughter of Marc Modena, who was the official radio operator aboard *L'Égaré II*. I met Mireille in the summer of 2016 at an event commemorating the 60th anniversary of the voyage. She was able to send me her personal copy of *L'argonaute*, her father's memoir. I knew this book existed, but I had been unable to find or purchase a copy (only 100 copies had been self-published).

Another exciting aspect was choosing to use comics to help tell the story of *L'Égaré II*. The illustrations allowed me to explore and visualize some of the aspects of the story that aren't recorded in photographs or on film — not just action-set pieces, like the clash with sharks, but also smaller moments, like those between a husband and a wife. They also give voice to some of the members of the crew who left little record of their experiences behind.

Details of the events in this volume are pieced together from a variety of sources, including interviews with individuals involved directly or indirectly with the original expeditions, as well as the written accounts of Marc and Henri. I also collected as much as I could of the newspaper and magazine coverage available from the era, going as far as Paris, France, to locate two 60-year-old periodicals that covered the voyage.

The end result is the most comprehensive and balanced account of this fascinating and underappreciated transatlantic voyage. I hope you enjoy it.

— Ryan Barnett, 2017

A NOTE ON *THE RAFTSMEN*

T HE POWER of a good piece of narrative non-fiction lies in its ability to present facts in an exciting and engaging way that embraces the art of storytelling.

Comics, on the other hand, have a special way of placing a reader at the heart of a story, immersing them in a world that may be otherwise hard to imagine. Comics often succeed in telling the kinds of stories that traditional bookmaking struggles to do.

The Raftsmen is a unique book and true hybrid of these two exciting genres. Ryan Barnett's exhaustive research, coupled with media coverage from the time and the photographic record created by Gaston Vanackere, creates an attractive and informative package. But the story really comes to life in the scripts Barnett wrote, as illustrated by Dmitry Bondarenko.

The comics included in *The Raftsmen* show life at sea for the crew of *L'Égaré II* as they were adrift for 89 days on the treacherous North Atlantic on a raft not even as long as a school bus. That's a reality few could adequately imagine. But Barnett's scripts go further, giving voice to those who had little representation in both the traditional media that initially covered the voyage and the first-hand accounts later created by the crew. Barnett highlights people like

Jeannine Beaudout, whose husband left her and their young daughter behind in Montreal, and RoseMarie Comeau-Maher, who was the raftsmen's only real conduit to the mostly English-speaking world of Halifax. Their stories are integral to the broader scope of the voyage of *L'Égaré II*.

Like the best Hollywood adaptations of true-life stories, the comics illustrated by Bondarenko necessitated some artistic licence. Dialogue, for the most part, is made up; details, like Gaston's stepping on the checkerboard after spotting a shark (see page 157) are added as compelling storytelling devices. What isn't made up are the underlying facts of each vignette. There's no way of knowing if Gaston really stepped on the checkerboard, but the boys *did* play checkers, and Gaston *did* scramble to get out in the dinghy to film the hunt.

The comics in this book acquaint readers with the members of the expedition in a way that would be difficult for words to render. The choice to portray Jose as pensive following a toast to the voyage in chapter 2 helps give him some dimension. Today, not much is known about Jose. After his departure from the raft due to seasickness he fades into obscurity. But here, in *The Raftsmen*, Jose is flesh and blood: a willing volunteer for adventure who may have been in over his head.

It is hard to achieve a completely balanced account in any story, but what Barnett (a documentary filmmaker by trade) has done here is separate fact from fiction to document this amazing story. It is an exciting, well-paced, multi-layered experience. I hope you enjoy crossing the North Atlantic as much as I have.

— Steve Cameron, editor

Crew of *L'Égaré II*

(The Raftsmen)

TOP LEFT
Henri Beaudout, captain

TOP RIGHT
Gaston Vanackere, cameraman

BOTTOM LEFT
Jose Martinez, cook

BOTTOM RIGHT
Marc Modena, radio man

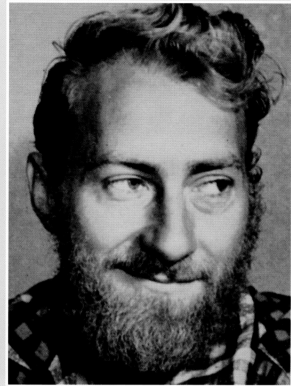

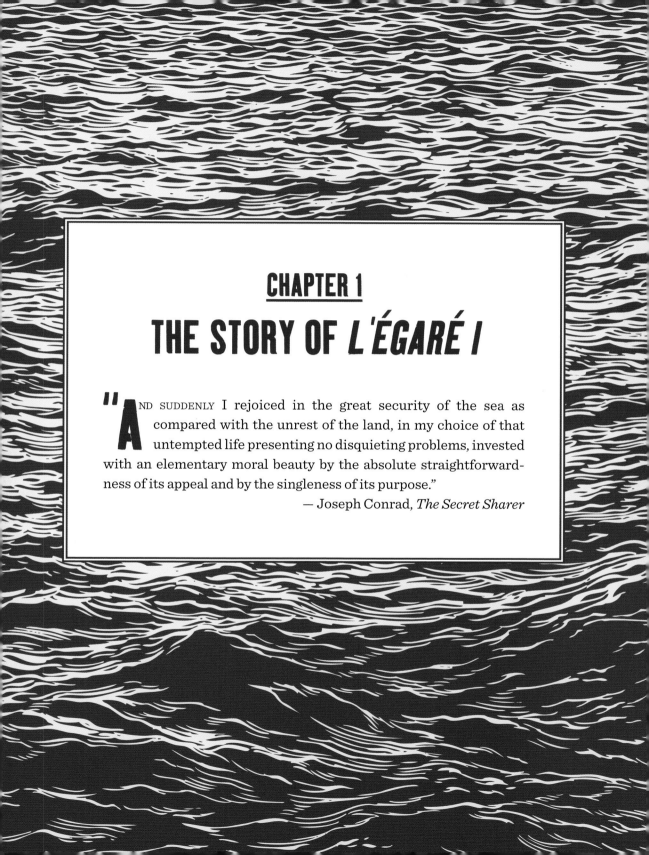

CHAPTER 1
THE STORY OF *L'ÉGARÉ I*

"AND SUDDENLY I rejoiced in the great security of the sea as compared with the unrest of the land, in my choice of that untempted life presenting no disquieting problems, invested with an elementary moral beauty by the absolute straightforwardness of its appeal and by the singleness of its purpose."

— Joseph Conrad, *The Secret Sharer*

THE CAPTAIN of the SS *Columbia* ordered passengers to stay in their cabins. The Greek ocean liner was passing through a late-March storm off the coast of Newfoundland, on its way from Cherbourg, France, to Halifax, Canada. The waters rose and fell, pitching the ship unpredictably. Twenty-four-year-old Henri Beaudout stood at the stern of the ship, testing his sea legs. As his wife, Jeannine, waited for him in their cabin, Henri drank in the beautiful ferocity of the North Atlantic. He had never seen anything like it before. The 700 souls aboard the *Columbia* were just travellers on a 8,500-ton cork at the mercy of the sea, Henri thought. The unbridled power of nature awoke something in him that day.

Henri as a toddler in Limousin, France.

Henri Beaudout was born on April 14, 1927, in Limousin, a region in central France, far from the sea. For the first years of his life, his aunt and uncle raised him because his parents worked as house staff for a wealthy family. "Papa Pierre," as Henri called his uncle, was a taxi driver, while "Maman Marie" ran a café. Young Henri used to stalk the café floor and help himself to a nip from the unfinished glasses of wine the patrons left behind.

As a boy, he went to the movies on Thursday afternoons to watch the latest adventures of Tarzan and Zorro. He dreamed of being a pilot. When he was six years old, Henri's parents returned for him. They were veritable strangers, and now he was expected to leave his beloved Papa Pierre and Maman Marie to live with them. Years later, Beaudout described this event as one of the early traumas of his life. The boy grew depressed and eventually fell ill. He caught diphtheria and then suffered from acute appendicitis.

"While I was in the hospital, doctors had to stop my biological parents from entering my room, because every time they did, I would throw a tantrum, which raised my temperature," Beaudout said. Eventually, with time, he grew to love his parents, though he never could bring himself to call them maman and papa.

Beaudout's adolescence was interrupted when German troops marched into southern France in November 1942, which expanded German occupation south across the country.

"You had to pick a side: either you collaborate or you resist,"

Henri at his First Communion.

Beaudout would later say of this time. "I was 16. And so I opted for the Resistance." He began his career smuggling identity papers to the Maquis du Limousin, one of the largest groups of French Resistance fighters. Colluding with a contact in the prefect's office, Henri would smuggle out papers with information about French citizens who now

Henri, left, in
military dress
with friend, date
unknown.

Henri as a member of the 107th Infantry Regiment (France).

BELOW: Henri can be seen in the middle, crouched and holding the gun.

lived abroad. These would be used to forge identification cards for Jews and escaped POWs. He did this without incident for a year, entering the office right under the noses of the occupying Germans and carrying the concealed documents to his liaison in the Resistance. Then, one day, his contact was arrested by the Gestapo, and Henri was forced to join the Maquis in the forest. Assuming the *nom de guerre* Bob Brumas, Beaudout fought as part of the Resistance until September 1944, when he joined the 107th Infantry Regiment. As he was getting set to deploy, he wrote to his parents:

"Dear Parents, when you receive this, I will be on the most extraordinary crusade of all time. Never, since the world has existed, has man had the occasion to participate in a mission as noble as this ... Hitler's machine is not yet destroyed. On the contrary, as its end approaches, its crimes intensify ... there are too many men still behind the barbed wire for me to disarm, now." As he wrote, these words once spoken by his father rang in his head: "The Allies don't need you to win the war."

Following the German surrender in May 1945, Beaudout spent the balance of his time with the 126th, sweeping Germany for Nazis in hiding. His tour of duty ended that December. He was a free man; at 18 years old, he was a civilian again. But France wasn't what it had been before the war — much of it was destroyed by bombings — and citizens who had lived under German occupation lashed out at those they saw as collaborators.

> "You had to pick a side: either you collaborate or you resist."
> — Henri Beaudout

"It was a period during which people had been deprived of food and all else," Beaudout recalled. "They had suffered, and they were letting off steam. They needed a scapegoat. We found women who had slept with Germans ... we took them, stripped them naked and shaved their heads — drew swastikas and other Nazi things on them, and made them march in the streets. People threw stones at them, spat on them — it was dreadful."

By his own account, Beaudout watched as those he knew to be collaborators and black marketers now drove American-made cars, did business with the Americans and retained the property they had acquired — unlawfully or unscrupulously — under the German occupation. "Meanwhile, I couldn't find a job," Beaudout said. The dishonest continued to prosper while the youths who had fought on behalf

Henri in his teenage years: left, pre-occupation and right, postwar.

Henri and Jeannine, far left of the middle row, celebrating with friends, likely in the late 1940s.

FACING PAGE:
Henri and Jeannine at their wedding in 1951.

of their country grew disillusioned. Beaudout dropped 50 pounds in this period and a black depression clouded his mind, as it had in the past. But unlike his boyhood trauma, time alone would not salve these wounds.

Henri Beaudout met Jeannine Lespagnol while commuting by train into the city. They were part of an extended group of young people who travelled together into Paris to work. They eventually broke off from the group, started dating and finally married in Paris on August 31, 1951. At the time, Henri was working for Air France — he had achieved his childhood dream of becoming a pilot, but he drew little satisfaction from it. France had too many bad memories — too many

Henri in the early 1950s as a draftsman with Hydro Quebec.

horrors — and the postwar rebuild was slow. The country held little promise for him and his new wife.

"After the war, France was partly destroyed from the bombings," Beaudout said. "The government was changing constantly. Between the strikes and changes of government, there was incredible instability in France. So we decided to try our luck in Canada." The *Columbia* arrived in Halifax on April 1, 1952, and the couple made their way to Montreal, drawn to the Francophonie presence in Quebec. Jeannine found work as a bookkeeper almost immediately;

Henri eventually found a position as a draftsman with Hydro Quebec.

Around this time, Hollywood was filling theatres with all sorts of war films; Billy Wilder's *Stalag 17* and Fred Zinnemann's *From Here to Eternity* were among the most popular.

For Beaudout, these films triggered memories from his service: "Every time I went to see one, I'd wake up later that night sweating buckets, shaking all over. I was having nightmares." He saw visions of friends who had been killed by his side — they begged Henri to save their lives. These dreams had started during the war and continued in the decade that followed.

"Eventually, I suffered a crisis of conscience. I had lost all my bearing and didn't know where I was." Beaudout sought medical advice, but the doctors couldn't find anything wrong with him. He had hoped that the move to Montreal would cure what had plagued him in France, but the pain just followed. "In this big city, one felt rather like an inconspicuous member of a huge herd," he wrote in his memoirs.

An idea gripped him at that time. It was frivolous, the kind of idea a young man might get when he wants to face anything but his own reality: he would start an explorers' club. This plan would take him away from the dull, anonymous city. The idea obsessed him for months.

Henri during the period of his life when he suffered a deep depression resulting from the war.

Montreal, 1952

Have a good day at work.

HONKKKKK

Good morning, Monsieur Deblois.

Madame Beaudout.

Seems there's always something going on out there, doesn't it?

So many car horns —

It's you and your husband! Kissing in the streets!

That may fly in France, but not here in Quebec!

Meanwhile ...

"I talked about it enthusiastically with my friends. But slowly their criticisms and arguments made it clear to me that though they thought an explorers' club a good idea, they could not see what qualifications I had to be its founder."

And then, on June 30, 1953, Jeannine gave birth to a little girl, Marie-Chantal Beaudout. It was the birth of his daughter that would prove to be the catalyst for action. "Chantal forced me to reflect, and I concluded that I needed to absolutely find a way to fill this void in me." To his thinking, he was still young enough to do something, to "break away from the herd" and return to his family, whether in triumph or failure.

Around this time, Henri came across a story in *Reader's Digest* about an Indigenous man who was found dying in his canoe on a beach in Portugal. As Beaudout remembers it, this had happened well before Jacques Cartier's first voyage across the Atlantic in 1534. Whether

Raft building at the marina in Longueuil, Quebec, in 1955.

this account is apocryphal or not, it gave Henri a renewed interest in the ocean. How is it that one man could have crossed an ocean on his own in such a modest vessel as a canoe? Surely he couldn't have done so under his own power. To find the answer to this question, Beaudout began studying ocean currents. An idea began to form in his head — an oceanic adventure that would be the solution to all his problems.

"I came to the conclusion that a skiff launched between the latitudes of 45 and 50 degrees north has to end up in Europe in 100 days at most." He would test this theory by designing a raft to carry him across the North Atlantic by the power of the winds and currents alone. Henri reckoned that if he could just make it to the Gulf Stream, the warm water currents would carry him the rest of the way. "If we didn't catch sight of Europe within 100 days, well, we might never be thirsty again."

L'Égaré I completely built and ready to sail in 1955.

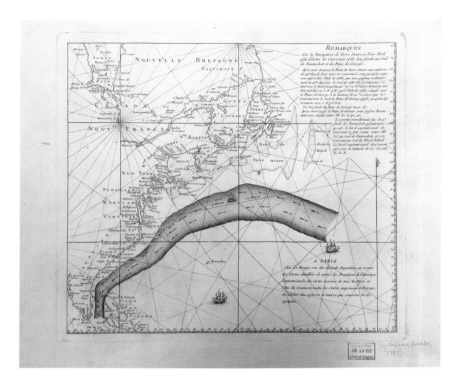

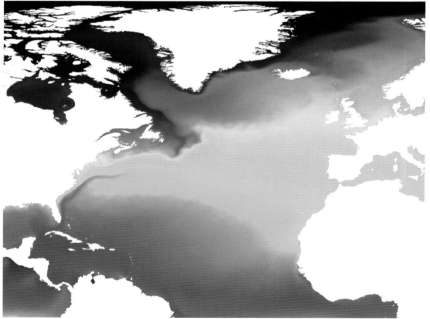

TOP: A second edition of the 1768 map created by Timothy Folger and Benjamin Franklin depicting the Gulf Stream; this edition was created in Paris by George-Louis le Rouge in 1785.

BOTTOM: A map of ocean temperatures in 2016, clearly depicting the Gulf Stream and its influence.

The story of the resulting voyage has not been told in any detail in over 60 years. Henri Beaudout would rather it be forgotten. It was an ill-conceived voyage plagued by a succession of unfortunate events.

Few are those, however, who conjure a grand idea to act upon and don't believe in it to the fullest. And Henri believed to his core that this voyage was good and necessary. In preparation for the journey he had spent months meticulously planning every aspect of the trip. He studied marine charts and sourced materials — he even paid a visit to a furniture-making school seeking advice on the best wood to make his raft with. Now a draftsman by trade, Henri drew up plans for his "floating fortress" — which amounted to little more than nine telephone poles lashed together by a length of manila rope. A large sail, about 24.7 metres (266 feet) square, would be the only means of propulsion other than the ocean currents. He planned everything down to the last detail. Every conversation he had was in service of collecting some sort of supply or tool he needed for the journey. Despite all his talking, there was still one thing that eluded him: he had no crew. Not one of Beaudout's friends was interested in embarking on such a foolish journey. Henri had to look outside his circle.

On April 3, 1955, *Le Petit Journal*, a working-class weekly paper, published the following headline: "In Search of a Brave Man to Cross the Atlantic Ocean on a Raft!" Henri had gone to the papers to find his crew. The article outlined his plans and included his address and phone number for "serious queries only." According to Henri, the next day, his phone was ringing off the hook with would-be sailors, from whom he identified what he thought were three suitable companions. Gaston Vanackere, a 29-year-old native of Lille, France, was the first to join, as the expedition's official photographer. Then came cook Bernard Sorieul, 24, of Lisieux in Normandy and radio operator Paul Lapointe, 30 years old and the sole Canadian on the team.

"Quartet of Bearded Adventurers Prepares to Shove Off This Week on Ocean Raft Excursion to Europe." So read the headline of a United Press article appearing in the *Daily Plainsman* on June 8, 1955. After several months of careful planning, Henri Beaudout and his crew of three willing-but-novice sailors were just about ready to set sail for Europe. Right from the start they were a target of derision from the newspapers. The French-language press called the trip a "poorer *Kon-Tiki.*" Thor Heyerdahl and the voyage of the *Kon-Tiki* was still fresh in people's minds at the time. It had made international headlines in 1947, and Heyerdahl's subsequent book on the expedition had been a bestseller. And just four years earlier, in 1951, *Kon-Tiki* won the Academy Award for best documentary feature. Heyerdahl's shadow loomed large over oceanic exploration.

> "I came to the conclusion that a skiff launched between the latitudes of 45 and 50 degrees north has to end up in Europe."
> — Henri Beaudout

The English press liked to focus on the crew's French-ness for comedic effect. The same United Press article quoted above, for instance, went on to claim that the "four bearded adventurers laid in supplies of cognac, cigarettes and pate de foie gras today aboard an untested raft." Another article from the time maintained that they packed cognac but forgot a compass. The men also reportedly carried some 4,000 cigarettes on board — about 10 cigarettes per day, per man, for their planned 100-day journey.

"All but Beaudout ... will make their wills," one newspaper reported in the lead-up to their departure. "They are unmarried and are leaving what savings remain from the $5,000 cost of the trip to the skipper's wife and two-year-old daughter, Chantal." On June 8, the day of their departure, Henri embraced Chantal and Jeannine for what could have been be the last time — one reporter wrote that

Jeannine "softly sobbed" during their goodbye. What followed was 70 days of bad luck.

Their plan was to launch from Montreal and travel up the St. Lawrence River to the Atlantic Ocean. Some three weeks earlier they had constructed the raft, 9 metres (30 feet) in length and made from British Columbian red cedar logs procured from Hydro Quebec. An article in the *Ottawa Journal* reported that "the raft was blessed and

Henri's last-ditch attempt to find crewmates for his 1955 attempt to cross the Atlantic Ocean on a raft appeared in the April 3, 1955, edition of *Le Petit Journal*.

christened with the 'Indian' name *Iotiapatonom* and the French name *L'Égaré* — both meaning 'the lost one.'"

The crew of "The Lost One" should have seen the writing on the wall from the start. First the vessel was "christened dry" because the Quebec Liquor Commission was closed on Sundays and no one had thought to buy champagne the previous day. Then the raftsmen were forced to drop anchor and wait out a storm for three days just 80 kilometres (50 miles) into their journey. *L'Égaré* and her crew would face countering winds most of the length of the St. Lawrence River, slowing their progress and sometimes even sending them in reverse. They hadn't even hit the ocean and things were bad. They were about to get a whole lot worse.

Around midnight on July 29, the crew of the SS *Wabana* spotted a flashing light in the dark waters of the northwest Atlantic. The large ore-carrier approached with caution and found Paul Lapointe and Bernard Sorieul alone in a dinghy. The two crewmen had temporarily left the safety of the raft in search of shore to replace some radio parts. They had miscalculated and rowed further out to sea instead. By the time they crossed paths with the *Wabana,* the men were down to a can of beef and a single cracker for rations. Lapointe told reporters shortly after this incident that he and Sorieul had nearly given up hope of rescue — their dinghy had begun to take on water. The chance encounter with the *Wabana* had saved them from certain drowning. The two men were brought to the French-owned islands of St-Pierre and Miquelon, located not far from Newfoundland, where they waited for the arrival of Henri and Gaston.

On August 4, the *Ottawa Journal* published an update on the good raft *L'Égaré*: Paul Sicaud, governor of St-Pierre and Miquelon, met with Lapointe and Sorieul and promised that he would reunite them with their raft, which by this point was floating off the coast of

THE DAILY NEWS

Vol. 62. No. 180.　　　ST. JOHN'S, NEWFOUNDLAND, MONDAY, AUGUST 1, 1955　　　(Price 5 cents)

In Chile

"Vision Of Terror" As Volcanoes Erupt

MARILYN BELL CAPTURES BRITISH ACCLAIM WITH PLUCKY CHANNEL SWIM

17-Year-Old Toronto Girl Is History's Youngest Conqueror of Straits

By RON EVANS
Canadian Press Staff Writer
DOVER, England (C.P.)—Seventeen-year-old Marilyn Bell captured the last 200 yards ashore today and became the youngest swimmer to conquer the English Channel.

The Toronto swimmer breasted the English coast at Abbotscliff, between Dover and Folkestone, at 2 p.m. (11:29 p.m. ADT), 14 hours and 36 minutes after setting out from Cap Gris Nez, France. The time was announced officially. She started at 1:52 a.m. 2:23 p.m. ADT.

Panicked People Flee For Safety But Many Caught

"Greatest Catastrophe Ever Witnessed"

VALDIVIA, Chile (A.P.)—Hundreds of persons carrying their exhausted children Sunday were reported fleeing from burning lava and rocks erupting from volcanoes Nilahue and Rininahue. At least 36 persons are missing presumably asphyxiated by poisonous fumes.

Thirty-five others were believed trapped without food in an area where the concentration of poisonous gases is heavy.

World News Briefs

VETERAN CYCLIST
MANSEAU, Que.—CP — Louis Boucher, 72, has cycled up to 12 and today, at 90, he has not lost his interest in the sport. Recently, he pedalled the 80 miles from this central Quebec town to Montreal in eight hours.

ALLY'S SONS SCORCHED
NICE, France (AP)—Two sons of Prince Aly Khan, Karim, 18, and Allim, 16, were slightly burned Saturday when a gasoline tank on their motor launch exploded.

SWIMMER HONORED
VICTORIA—CP — Bert Thomas, first person to swim the Strait of Juan de Fuca, was honored recently by being the third person ever made a freeman of Victoria.

REDS CHARGE SPYING
BERLIN (AP)—The Communist party newspaper Neues Deutschland says Manfred Lagen, 35-year-old leader of a right-wing group in West Germany, has been arrested on espionage charges.

COMMISSION ADVISOR
VICTORIA—CP — Chartered accountant A. P. Foster of Vancouver has been appointed adviser to Chief Justice Gordon Sloan.

REES HARRIMAN CHOICE
NEW YORK (AP)—Vice-President Richard Nixon, asked by a reporter who he thinks will be the Democratic nominee for president next year, said: "From what I've heard, it looks like Averell Harriman of New York seems to be gaining strength."

TOO LATE
DURHAM, England — CP —Frank Brockwell's newly-planted garden was dug up by excited gardeners buying a power plug.

DROP TRAVEL TAX
WASHINGTON (AP)—The House of Representatives passed and sent to the Senate Saturday night a bill to repeal the 10-per-cent tax on travel from the United States to nearby countries—Canada, Mexico, Central America and the Caribbean area.

TURPIN'S TAVERN TO GO
PLAINSTOW, Eng. (Reuters)—The Green Gate, a 325-year-old tavern said to have been patronized by highwayman Dick Turpin, is to be pulled down. It was badly damaged by a bomb during the war and will be replaced by a new building.

Russia Ready To Co-Operate On Research In Outer Space

By SIDNEY WEILAND
MOSCOW (Reuters)—The Soviet Union's top interplanetary investigator, A. G. Karpenko said Saturday Russia is ready in principle to co-operate in outer-space research with other nations.

Business Spotlight

Easing Monetary Controls Paves Way For English Branches

OTTAWA (C.P.)—Easing of Britain's currency controls is paving the way for British industries to open branches in Canada.

COASTAL TRADE

Ban Foreign Ships By 1957 Asked By Canada S.S. Company

MONTREAL (C.P.)—Canada Steamship Lines has urged that Canada's coastal shipping trade be limited after Jan. 1, 1957, to ships built in Canada.

S.S. Wabana Rescues Men Of "I'Egare"

SYDNEY, N.S. (CP)—The radio-operator of the raft, l'Egare, the Lost One, Paul Lapointe told Sunday how the chance appearance of the ore-carrier Wabana saved them from possible drowning.

Describe First Atomic Powered Electric Plant

OTTAWA (C.P.)—A preliminary description of Canada's first electricity-producing atomic power plant has been released by Atomic Energy of Canada Ltd., the crown company charged with atomic research in this country.

Heiress To Huge Fortune Takes Own Life

NEW YORK (AP)—Miss Alice Belmont, one of the heiresses of the gigantic fortune of banker August Belmont, Jr., was found dead Saturday in her gas-filled Manhattan apartment, Police listed the death as apparent suicide.

Caught 19 Fish On One Hook

BOURNEMOUTH, Eng. (AP)—Members fish caught on the same hook at the same time in the claim of Edward Knott.

INSIDE

2—Big Dipper science at Lorin
5—Boy Roberts News
6—Trinity News
8—"Hansen's Second Hell"—editorial
11—Women's News and Chit Chat
14—Farm Page
10, 11—Sport
22—Movie reviews

WEATHER

Cloudy, scattered showers. Little warmer. High today: 72.

Nfld. Skies

MONDAY, August 1st.

Sunrise .... 6:27 a.m.
Sunset .... 7:37 p.m.

TIDES
High ...... 6:00 a.m. 5:54 p.m.
Low .... 11:35 a.m. 11:55 p.m.

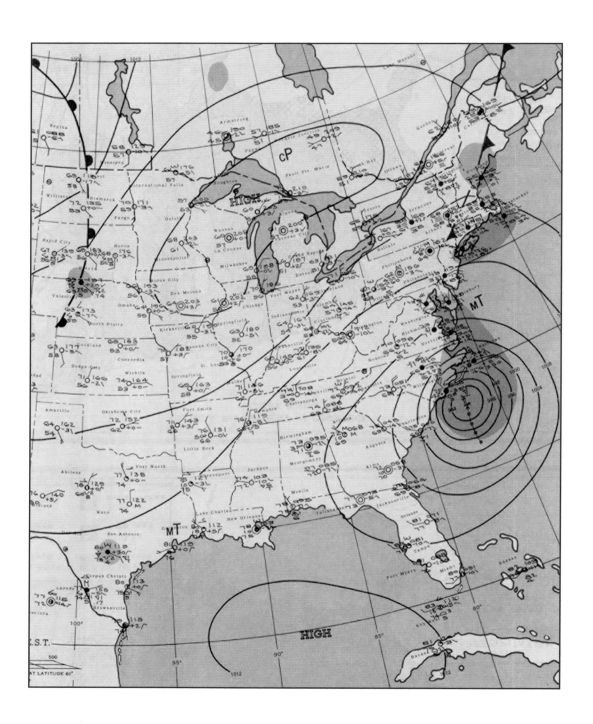

Port aux Basques, Newfoundland. He confirmed that once the crew was back together, their raft would be towed out into the Atlantic and set adrift toward the Gulf Stream. However, as Hurricane Connie moved her way up the eastern seaboard, conditions for the raftsmen worsened. Countering winds had plagued them across the St. Lawrence River, slowing them to a crawl and sometimes undoing a day's progress. Now, they were faced with gale-force winds that could tear apart their craft. Governor Sicaud had a change of heart — he still reunited the sailors when the raft made it from Port aux Basques to the French-owned islands, but adjusted the plans to return the raft and its crew to Canada instead. Their journey was effectively over.

Faced with this news, Henri made two tough decisions as captain: the first was to leave Bernard Sorieul in St-Pierre and Miquelon. The young man had been suffering from terrible seasickness, and Henri decided it was time their cook took his leave. Henri then set about a plan to defy the orders of the governor. Colluding with the skipper of the *Langlade* — the ship charged with returning *L'Égaré* to

By the time they crossed paths with the *Wabana*, the men were down to a can of beef and a single cracker for rations.

Canadian shores — Henri plotted their escape. As the *Langlade* towed *L'Égaré* toward Newfoundland, Henri would cut the tow rope and set their raft and the now three-man crew back adrift and on course for Europe. Meanwhile, for his part, the skipper of the *Langlade* would claim that they lost the raft in the fog. And so it went — on August 9th, the men were once again heading in the direction of the Gulf Stream. But in a week's time, *L'Égaré* would shake hands with Connie.

Peter's River, Newfoundland,
3 a.m., August 17, 1955

Gaston will be okay.

Later

Do you know where your raft wrecked?

Eastward, I think.

It was foggy, but we followed a sheep's trail here from the shore.

Our dory only fit two, so we threw Charlotte in with us and left Gaston behind.

Charlotte?

Our cat.

My husband will find your friend. You boys get some rest.

I was on the tiller that morning.

A great wall of fog surrounded us.

We were on a collision course.

BRACE YOURSELVES!

KRRRKKKK

It's bad, Henri.

6 a.m., August 17, 1955

We'll be home soon as we can.

I hope their mate is still alive.

We must be getting close.

Jeez.

Our radio was damaged. We couldn't call for help ...

... We had to go.

Gaston stayed with the raft. I knew I could count on him to the limit.

We scaled the shoreline cliff.

I had nothing left in the tank ...

... only a belief in my friend.

AHOY!

MONTREAL

ST-PIERRE AND MIQUELON

PETER'S RIVER,
NEWFOUNDLAND

VOYAGE OF *L'ÉGARÉ I*

June 8, 1955, to August 16, 1955
- Days on the raft: 70
- Nautical miles travelled: 702 nm (1,300 km/809 mi)
- Average distance per day: 11 nm (20 km/13 mi)

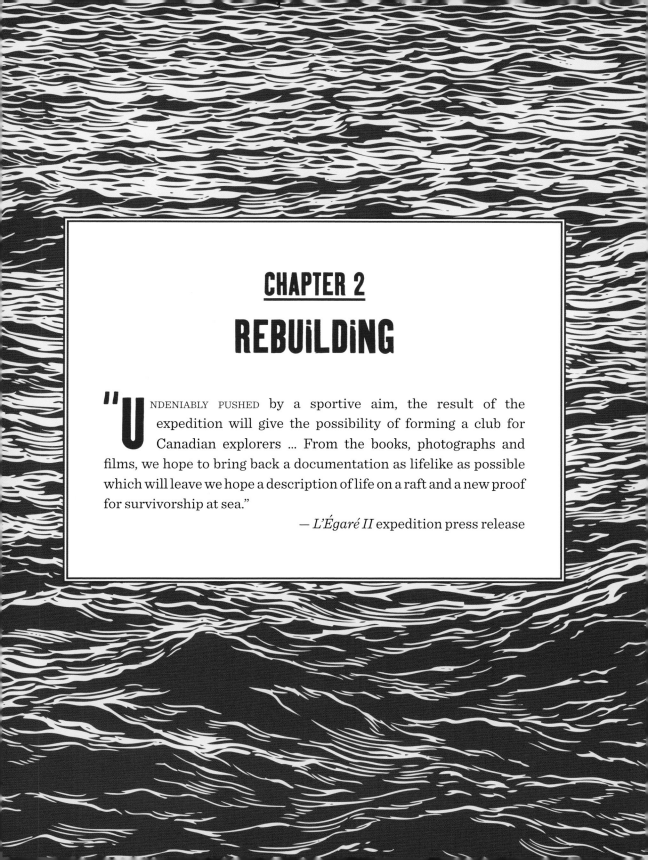

CHAPTER 2
REBUILDING

"UNDENIABLY PUSHED by a sportive aim, the result of the expedition will give the possibility of forming a club for Canadian explorers ... From the books, photographs and films, we hope to bring back a documentation as lifelike as possible which will leave we hope a description of life on a raft and a new proof for survivorship at sea."

— *L'Égaré II* expedition press release

THESE WERE the concluding words of the expedition press release distributed prior to the departure of *L'Égaré II*. A second attempt was inevitable — just two days after the wreck of *L'Égaré, The Daily News* out of St. John's reported the following: "The men are determined that they will try it again next year. But this time, they said, we shall try it from Halifax and not Montreal." Upon revisiting the site of the crash the morning after, Henri Beaudout had known he could not let things end that way.

"I had just achieved the opposite of what I'd set out to do," he said. "I justified my detractors. If I had stopped there, what would my life have been like after?"

Gaston Vanackere had managed to save the camera equipment, but little else of their gear and supplies remained, either having been

Henri appears on the popular CBC show *Rendez-vous avec Michelle,* hosted by Michelle Tisseyre.

lost at sea or reclaimed by local fishermen. Bernard Sorieul had left them, and Paul Lapointe was unsure about embarking on another journey after the disaster of the first. But Vanackere swore his allegiance to Beaudout. If they were to plan another expedition, though, they would be starting from scratch. They would need more men, nine more telephone poles, a sailmaker, tools and supplies. First and foremost, they needed money, so they returned to work in Montreal.

Almost as soon as he arrived back in town, Beaudout received a call from a friendly stranger. Marc Modena was a French émigré working as a house painter in Montreal. He had arrived in Canada just a few months earlier, landing in Halifax and carrying just $25 in his pocket. *L'Égaré* had first piqued his interest when he saw Henri on TV just prior to its June departure. By all accounts, Modena was an entertaining and sympathetic fellow, built sturdy and low to the ground. He had long dreamed of the kind of sea adventure described by Beaudout in that interview and in the subsequent newspaper coverage of the expedition. Fear wasn't something that plagued Marc Modena.

"I understand that you're going to leave again," he said to Beaudout on the phone that night. "I would be very proud to go with you." It warmed Henri's heart, this vote of blind confidence, and confirmed his resolve to resume the voyage.

"I tell you what," Henri said. "Give me some time to regroup — I see you've been bitten, but call me again in two months." Modena waited, and in exactly two months' time, he called back and found out that Paul Lapointe had dropped out of the next expedition. By October 1955, Marc Modena was the newest member of the team. He called his parents with the news.

"I think you're crazy, and I tell you, this Beaudout is also crazy," his dad told him.

John Paterson,
OBE, at a harbour,
likely in the late
1950s.

In December 1955, Beaudout took a reconnaissance run to Halifax. Of his many goals, one was to obtain lumber for the construction of the new raft. Armed with a letter of recommendation, Henri met with a friend of his Montreal boss at Hydro Quebec, an engineer from the Maritime Telephone and Telegraph Company (MT&T). In search of red cedar logs, Henri had hoped to procure them from the phone company, similar to how he had sourced the logs for his first raft from Hydro Quebec. Unfortunately, the MT&T only used white cedar logs, which were smaller, less sturdy and far from ideal. However, Henri didn't leave empty handed. The engineer directed him to the Dartmouth Marine Slip. He recommended that Beaudout meet with Mr. Paterson, the superintendent of the shipyard. This piece of advice would be the crucial turning point in the story of *L'Égaré II*.

John Paterson, OBE, was born in 1887 in Wick, Caithness, at the northeastern tip of Scotland. He came to Canada following the First World War and started managing the Dartmouth Slip in 1921. The men who worked under him at the shipyard called him "the Super." According to a 1958 newspaper article that covered his retirement from the yards, Mr. Paterson was often referred to as "Dartmouth's No. 1 citizen." For Beaudout, having a man of Mr. Paterson's largesse and connections would prove invaluable. The Super agreed to let Henri and his crew use the shipyard and whatever tools they needed to build their raft.

> "I think you're crazy, and I tell you, this Beaudout is also crazy."
> — Mr. Modena Sr.

Mr. Paterson was known as a sober man. Why would he invite this crew, who had little chance of success, to disrupt his yard? Perhaps Henri's pitch sold him — he got swept up in the young man's enthusiasm and conviction for this scheme. But according to Paterson's own daughter, Joan Fluelling, he never once spoke to her about Beaudout or *L'Égaré II*. So how swept up could he have been? In fact, Joan sees the decision to open his yard to the expedition as somewhat out of character for her father. During the Great War, Mr. Paterson had been charged to run two key shipyards — a duty that proved so mentally taxing that "when he heard people shouting that war was over, he just went blank. Didn't know where he was," his daughter Joan recalled. Mr. Paterson suffered a nervous breakdown. It's possible that he saw something of his own experience in Beaudout's wounded eyes that afternoon.

Henri returned to Montreal. The expedition still needed a lot of help and one more member, but meeting Mr. Paterson had filled him with a renewed confidence.

The final member of the crew would be Jose Martinez. He drove a taxi in Montreal and had befriended Gaston during the preparations for the first expedition. When he expressed interest in joining them on the second, the matter was settled and the team was in place.

Members of the Crew:
HENRi BEAUDOUT, native of LiMOGES, chief and captain of the expedition, 29 years old.
GASTON VANACKERE, native of LiLLE, cameraman, 30 years old.
MARC MODENA, native of FRÉJUS, radio man, 29 years old.
JOSE MARTiNEZ, native of GRENOBLE, cook, 34 years old.
— *L'Égaré II* expedition press release

Mr. Paterson, meanwhile, was proving himself indispensable. Just weeks after meeting Beaudout, he stumbled upon a timber merchant who just happened to have nine large trunks of British Columbian red cedar in Dartmouth. Mr. Lehman of Lehman Lumber had been sitting on the logs for some time, so when Henri approached him to purchase the wood, he was only too eager to make a deal. He even agreed to cut the cedars to size and deliver them to the slip. Mr. Paterson agreed to store the wood until March, when the crew planned to return to Halifax and begin construction.

In the lead-up to March, the boys sourced equipment and other materials they would need for their journey. They couldn't afford a chronometer, but Vanackere had managed to swipe the sextant from the wreckage of *L'Égaré* — so navigation was covered. They were able to source a BC-654, an old military radio, from a local Quebec dealer. A bulky piece of equipment that dated back to the Second World War, it weighed 22 kilograms (50 pounds) and was powered by a hand crank. Modena, the radio operator, had been in the French navy and knew how to transmit Morse code. However, he wasn't proficient enough to decode it. They found a sailmaker to make a new sail, 5.8 × 4.3 metres (19 × 14 feet), made from Egyptian cotton, and Paquette Ltd. of Quebec donated all the kitchen supplies they needed for their journey. By the second week of February, the crew had bought a van, and by March 1, 1956, they'd packed it up and were off to Halifax to start construction on *L'Égaré II*.

From 1928 to 1971, Pier 21 operated as the entrance into Canada. More than 1 million immigrants, arriving by ocean liner, passed through its terminal. In 1956, RoseMarie Comeau was just 20 years old. Born into a large Acadian family, she grew up very poor in Pointe-de-l'Église, a small fishing community some 250 kilometres (155 miles) from Halifax. Being fluent in French, she was able to secure a summer job in the big city as a service representative with the MT&T. When immigrants landed in Halifax, they went to MT&T to call their families back home or those waiting for them in Montreal, New York — wherever it may be. It was part of Comeau's duties to assist these new arrivals.

One afternoon in December 1955, RoseMarie received a call from one of the engineers working on the second floor of MT&T's Hollis Street headquarters.

"I hear you speak French," he said.

"Yes," she replied.

"Please come right away. There is a Frenchman in my office, and I have no idea what he wants."

When RoseMarie entered the engineer's office, she met Henri Beaudout for the first time. Henri had come to see the engineer on the recommendation of his boss in Montreal, and he was hoping to procure red cedar logs for his raft. It was RoseMarie who translated the engineer's disappointing news that the MT&T used white cedar, which wasn't suitable. It was also RoseMarie who directed him to Mr. Paterson.

Three months later, in March 1956, RoseMarie got another call from the second floor: "That Frenchman is back in my office, and he's brought friends."

"Do you need me up there?" she asked.

"Yes, quickly!" So RoseMarie ran upstairs and found all four raftsmen waiting for her.

"We don't really want anything from your friend," Henri told her, speaking in French. "We were looking for you. We need your help." By this point, they had discovered that Halifax was not like Montreal, and almost nobody was bilingual. Communicating with folks around town was always difficult, and they were having a great deal of trouble obtaining supplies. Beaudout hoped that RoseMarie would be willing to help them as an interpreter. "Of course, we can't pay you anything," he finished.

The money didn't make a difference to RoseMarie — after all, something like this didn't happen every day in Halifax. She signed on to be the secretary of the expedition, a title more reflective of the times than it was of her duties. They called her at work and at home to speak with merchants. On weekends, she went down to the slip, where they were working, to translate their mail and type correspondence. Every time the crew encountered a problem, RoseMarie was their first call.

"I knew Henri was the leader from the word 'go.' He just had that air about him," RoseMarie said in an interview years later. "I thought he was very cool, smoking all the time." She was quite fond of both Gaston and Marc, while Jose struck her as a little out of step with the other three. He was quieter, "a little older, maybe more mature."

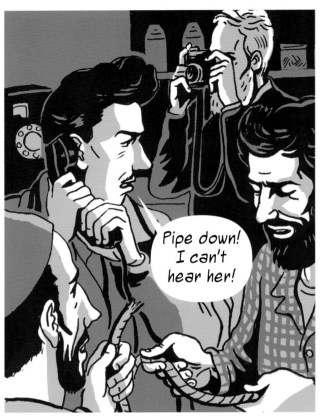

Pipe down! I can't hear her!

Hi, Rosie!

Shh!

We're calling from the hardware store ...

... I need you to tell the gentleman that we want 7,000 feet of cordage.

That's a lot of rope! He must think you're bonkers.

Put him on the line. I'll explain everything.

The Raftsmen lash logs together in the Dartmouth Slip to form the base of *L'Égaré II*.

True to his word, Mr. Lehman had the logs cut to length and delivered them to the Dartmouth Slip. However, work was far from complete. All nine logs still had to be planed to a uniform half-metre (22-inch) diameter. With no planer available, this work was done by hand using axes and chisels. In the two months leading up to their planned departure on May 19, the men worked 12-hour days constructing their raft. At night, they retired to a modest yacht, the *Atomic*, which Mr. Nelson, the director of the shipyard, had offered them — another example of Haligonian hospitality. Marc made dinner for the crew and maybe a local or two. Another Frenchman working nearby them in the yard had taken note of their obvious lack of funds, and he often stopped in after a day's work with a bottle of rum or something equally warming to drink.

Beaudout's plans for the raft called for no nails, no screws, no modern hardware of any kind — the raft would be bound together with rope. Working outside in the cool, early spring, Henri, Gaston, Marc and Jose painstakingly chipped and carved the logs to the desired diameter. They chiselled deep notches down the length of each post, in which the bindings would rest. Too heavy to manoeuvre on land, the trunks had to be pushed into the harbour and assembled in the water. While balancing on top of the floating logs, one man hammered away with a mallet to soften the frozen manila rope as two others pulled the binding knots tight with all of their might. Over 1,829 metres (6,000 feet) of rope was used in the construction of *L'Égaré II*, at a cost of $1,000, roughly 20 per cent of their entire budget for the trip. From an account of the North Atlantic expedition:

CONSTITUTION OF THE RAFT *L'ÉGARÉ II*

- **9 LOGS OF BRITISH COLUMBIA RED CEDAR of 30 feet in length and an average diameter of 22 inches from the base of which the attachments are uniquely manila rope of 1 inch and ¼ in diameter.**
- **6 CROSSBARS ALSO OF RED CEDAR joined in the bulk by means of an axe: 10 feet in diameter, 17 feet long constitute the main binding of logs and also support the floor of the cabin; cabin constructed of laths, basket woven by us with care, which is 4 feet high, 10 feet long and 7 feet wide.**
- **2 MASTS IN V SHAPE are 25 feet long (local light wood).**
- **6 MOBILE BOOMS of 6 feet long and 1 foot wide assure the drift; one rudder in the shape of an oar, the direction.**

— *L'Égaré II* expedition press release

Drinking seawater can be deadly. Our kidneys are only able to produce urine that is less salty than saltwater, so, when one drinks seawater, the body has to urinate more water than was actually consumed in order to expel the high amounts of sodium taken in. This leads to muscle cramps, dry mouth and other symptoms of dehydration. Blood flow to the brain and organs is affected and could eventually lead to a coma, organ failure and death.

Henri Beaudout had calculated that their journey across the North Atlantic would take 100 days. If they wanted to avoid the fate of the Indigenous man washed up in his canoe on the Portuguese beach, they would need to bring freshwater with them. This was 1956, when buying water in a portable container was futuristic, so Beaudout had to devise a way to transport the amount required to sustain life on the raft. The plan was to carry freshwater in 50-millilitre (1.7-ounce) cans, which they would ration out each day: three parts freshwater, one part seawater. Of course, the men would have to make the cans, no small feat in and of itself. The raftsmen needed to find a facility that could sterilize the water and then fill and seal the cans ready for transport. It was early April by this point, and their May 19 departure date was looming. To solve this problem, Beaudout would do something that he hadn't done since he was a wee child in Limoges: he turned to the Church.

Henri Beaudout knew that many orders of Catholic priests often did all kinds of work outside of the duties of their faith. He contacted a local Halifax priest and inquired about whether he knew anyone in the church who might be able to sterilize and can water for their journey. The father promised Henri that he would think about it and get in touch if something useful came to mind. A couple of weeks passed before Henri finally received word from this priest, who had contacted the Dominion Molasses plant in Halifax. He told Henri that if he brought one of his cans to the plant, they could tell him immediately whether their machinery could seal them. Optimistic, as was his character, Henri went down that day and the factory confirmed that they could indeed do the job.

With half his water problem solved, Beaudout turned to a local dairy — surely, he thought, they had to sterilize all their equipment. Perhaps they could sterilize a bit of water for a few boys in need. As it turned out, the farmer couldn't have been more agreeable: "Be here before 7 a.m. each day, before I have to start my work, and I'll sterilize your water." He would place the sterilized water in a big container that the boys could drive over to the molasses plant for canning. For his part, the manager of the factory put all the resources he could into finishing the job as swiftly as possible. By April 26, the water problem was solved.

Raft Stores

110 pounds potatoes
34 pounds rice
10 pounds flour
10 pounds dried beans
17 sliced and toasted loaves of bread
70 small jars of meat paste
40 cans of soup
13 cans of corned beef
10 jars of pickled pork tongues
4 cans of pork loaf
3 cans of sausages
50 cans of apple juice
100 cans freshwater

By late April, the raft was coming together. As it began to look more seaworthy (only a matter of opinion, as some would never think it looked seaworthy), the public scrutiny of the men and doubts about the expedition began to rise. At one point, early on, the crew had approached the French consul in Halifax to ask him for assistance and to provide a flag, so the four Frenchmen could fly their country's colours from the mast of their vessel as they sailed across the North Atlantic. On April 26, Henri received a call from the French consul. Henri later wrote of this call: "I hoped he might have some good news for me. But he told me he was telephoning to let me know that he had consulted a number of people ... and, as a result of what he had learnt from them, he had decided that his conscience would not allow him to give me the flag of my country to fly from the masthead; nor could he offer any assistance of any other kind." Among the people the consul knew in both the Royal Canadian Navy and the French navy, opinion was unanimous: the four raftsmen didn't have chance at success.

On that very day, Beaudout would encounter a similar attitude from a Canadian Forces chaplain. Henri had gone to the man hoping to borrow a spare rubber dinghy from the army's stores. He had hoped the Catholic chaplain would assist him, just as a priest had helped him with the water cans. However, the two holy men were perhaps not cut from the same cloth. The chaplain told Henri, showing very little hesitation, that the army had nothing to give or lend to his expedition.

"Your chances of survival are one in a thousand," he told Henri.

It was an argument that didn't make much sense to Beaudout. They were embarking on the expedition regardless. If this "man of God" was so certain that they would perish, was it not his duty to ensure they had every possible chance of survival? Wouldn't providing a dinghy — a literal life raft — be the Godly thing to do? Still, Beaudout ended the day flag-less and dinghy-less.

It was now early May. The men were working in the shipyard,

Henri stands on the port side toward the stern of *L'Égaré II*. To his right is the canvas covered cabin; behind him, hanging off the stern, is the rudder.

putting together the lattice cabin. A sergeant from the RCMP and a couple of local police constables approached them and asked to see the skipper of the expedition. Henri made himself known. The sergeant produced a pen and a questionnaire from his pocket and began asking questions. He wanted to know Henri's full name and address. He wanted to know the names of Marc, Gaston and Jose and where they lived. Having grown up in occupied France, this scene was all too familiar to Beaudout. In his broken English, he interrupted to ask what exactly their goal was with this interview.

"I want to know exactly who you are and where you live, so that when you disappear, I will be able to report who has disappeared and from where," the sergeant responded without guile. "That's all."

It was a frank response, one that amused Henri, Marc, Gaston and Jose. By this point, lack of faith from outsiders was just a way of life for them. It ran like water off a raft's deck. It was enough that they had a small but merry band of supporters: Mr. Paterson and RoseMarie. Also, shortly after being rebuffed by the French consul, Beaudout had

The raftsmen (from left to right), Jose, Marc, Henri and Gaston, stand on *L'Égaré II* during construction.

approached Henry Hicks, the premier of Nova Scotia, who was only too glad to provide them with a Nova Scotian flag for their mast. And sweet RoseMarie would eventually do one even better.

Even though several of her friends had told her she was taking a risk by spending time with the four Frenchmen, she had become quite close to them. She spent most weekends at the slip or around town assisting the crew however she could. She ate with them from time to time. To her, the men seemed carefree, and that rubbed off on her.

"I was just a young country girl," she said. "I felt they could do it because they were so determined." She had witnessed for herself the amount of preparation that each man put into the trip. "I had read the story of Thor Heyerdahl, and I thought, if Thor could do it, Henri could, too." At the time, RoseMarie didn't know about the first attempt that had ended in a wreck. Her faith was to remain unshaken by such knowledge.

Over some of those dinners on the *Atomic*, she asked the men about the war. She remembered rationing as a young girl — butter, sugar, gas, tires. Her father could buy gas and tires because he was driving himself and three others to the shipyards to build corvettes, but their neighbours had been forced to put their cars up on blocks. The Bedford Basin would be full of ships at night, but by morning, not one would remain. U-boats stationed just outside Sambro, Nova Scotia, would pick off ships as they went in or out of port. But the Frenchmen didn't want to talk about the war. They just told her it was terrible and they didn't have much to eat.

FACING PAGE:
L'Égaré II, ready to set sail in late May, 1956.

"I could tell they didn't want to discuss it very much, so we didn't."

The journey was the goal. And if France didn't want *L'Égaré II* flying its flag, RoseMarie was only too proud to see them fly the Acadian flag. Of course, at that time, you couldn't just buy an Acadian flag in a store, so she sewed one and gave it to the crew. They would have their beloved blue, white and red, only with the addition of the yellow star to symbolize Mary, patron saint of mariners. The Stella Maris would

Gaston rows out to sea in the dinghy to take photos of the raft from afar.

see them safely through the rough sea.

In the lead-up to the raft's departure, Haligonians pooled their money and bought the crew the rubber dinghy they so badly needed. Though many of them were likely skeptical about the trip, they had grown fond of the four Frenchmen, following their exploits of the past two months as reported by the Halifax *Chronicle Herald,* and they wanted to give them every chance of surviving their trip. For Gaston, this also meant he could film the raft from afar while out at sea. This new dinghy would add a great deal of production value to the documentary that he'd started upon their arrival in Halifax.

Another gift arrived on the heels of their new flags and the dinghy: friends from Quebec had sent by train two kittens to take along on the journey. Every great expedition needs a mascot: Ernest Shackleton brought an Alsatian named Query and a kitten named Questie to the Antarctic, and the *Kon-Tiki* had a parrot, that is, until the bird flew away. Of course, *L'Égaré* had had Charlotte, and *L'Égaré II* would have Puce and Guiton. So it was to be: four men and two kittens on board nine logs, lashed together by rope.

CREW OF RAFT READY FOR DEPARTURE AFTER THREE WEEKS SEARCH FOR TOW
—*Chronicle Herald,* May 24, 1956

In a CBC interview in anticipation of their departure, Beaudout made the mistake of referring to the kittens, which sent the local SPCA representatives apoplectic. They feared the cats would drown — a silly assertion to Beaudout, who thought the cats would not drown just as long as they stayed on the raft. That was his plan for survival as well. The SPCA demanded that the kittens be left on shore. Perhaps they were being reactionary or perhaps they knew from history what happened to most voyage mascots: Query, Shackleton's Alsatian, was swept overboard; Questie's fate is lost to history; and for anyone who doesn't know the average flight range of a parrot, it's not likely that the bird found its way to shore from the middle of the Pacific.

On May 24, 1956, the *Chronicle Herald* reported that the RCMP paid another visit to the raft in search of the cats: "Police said that the search for the two young kittens was made after numerous complaints ... about the subjection of the pair to the perils of the Atlantic. Jose told reporters that they had given the kittens to friends for safekeeping while they were away."

By the middle of May, preparations for the voyage were complete, and not a moment too soon. All that remained of their $5,000 budget was $3, and if they didn't cast off soon, they would be the first mariners to starve in port. But the final piece was still missing. For three weeks, the crew had searched in vain for a boat to tow them out of port, but no fisherman was willing, fearing liability should the men drown, as they almost assuredly would. Their May 19 departure date came and went with still no means of getting the raft to the ocean.

Here again, Mr. Paterson and the shipyard intervened to help the crew of *L'Égaré II*. Eager to get the boys on

Captain Cyril Henneberry.

their way — they had only a small window when the weather might be calm enough for a safe voyage — Mr. Paterson called on Cyril Henneberry for assistance. Henneberry captained a small fishing vessel called the *Promise*, which he crewed with three of his brothers. Their ship was in the slip for repairs on the morning of May 23, when Henneberry was asked to help.

According to the captain himself, he never considered the liability: "I just did it to help out the shipyard," he later said. "Of course, that would get me more favours over there." Henneberry had heard of the *Kon-Tiki* — he had once spent a week in Norway looking at new fishing vessels — but when he saw *L'Égaré II,* he didn't think much of the Frenchmen's chances. "I thought it was sort of foolish, m'self, especially on that contraption." Nevertheless, he committed to towing the 10-ton raft some 50 kilometres (30 miles) out to sea. They would depart the following day, May 24, 1956. That night, the raftsmen had their final dinner on the *Atomic*, and RoseMarie joined them.

Captain Cyril Henneberry (top) and the crew of the *Promise*.

Halifax, Nova Scotia,
May 23, 1956

There she goes to see her Frenchmen again.

Can you believe her parents let her take such risks?

RoseMarie!

I brought bread.

Good girl!

Some wine?

Hi Rosie!

Later

That's it for the wine.

But we haven't even toasted!

We'll just have to drink the champagne!

THUMP

That champagne is for the raft christening!

So?

Drinking it would be bad luck!

Press and well-wishers gathered at the Dartmouth Slip to bid adieu to Henri, Gaston, Marc and Jose. Mr. Paterson was there to wish them a safe voyage. He was certain that the boys would land in Scotland — he had said so to each of them, several times.

The crew asked RoseMarie to do the honours of christening the ship. A priest had visited the night before, at RoseMarie's request, to bless the vessel. The champagne bottle had been refilled with ginger ale and recorked — anyone outside their circle was none the wiser to the liberties taken the night before. The news cameras would capture the spectacle regardless of the contents of the bottle. Standing on the dock, RoseMarie threw the bottle against the log raft, at which point it bounced off the deck. She made a second attempt. Same result. A CBC cameraman then tossed a crowbar onto the deck.

"Hit the metal, that should break it," he told her.

Her third try was a success, spraying ginger ale all over the logs. A keen eye can spot the metal bar in the film footage from that morning. Friends they made during their time in Halifax had packed the boys sandwiches, so they would not have to worry about cooking on their first night at sea. Newsmen asked them the inevitable question: "Why? Why do this?" Perhaps they hadn't read RoseMarie's press release or perhaps they just didn't believe that establishing an explorers' club was worth the risk. It had been arranged that the crew of *L'Égaré II* would collect aquatic specimens to be studied at the University of Montreal, but this was only the byproduct of a trip already in progress — "Hey, while you're out there, can you bring us back some plankton?"

Marc, left, and Henri, middle, discuss radio communication with Aaron Solomon, who would be their Halifax radio contact while the raft was still in range.

DICUSS RADIO CONTACT — The radioman and captain of the ocean going raft L'Egare, "The Wanderer", are shown above as they confer with Aaron Solomon of Dartmouth on the frequency they will used in transmitting their daily messages to him and other members of the Maritime Radio Network. On Mr. Solomon's left are Marc Modena, radioman, and Captain Henri Beaudot, who will also do the navigating. (Conrod Photo).

Perilous Journey Planned By Four At Dartmouth

Of course, there was the loftier answer, the "Thor Heyerdahl" answer that Beaudout often repeated: the navigational theory that you could float a vessel between the 45th and 50th parallels and it would naturally drift from North America to Europe. This hypothesis also appears in Henri Beaudout's 1957 account of the voyage; however, it isn't often repeated in the press coverage from 1956. Certainly it was the crux of the voyage, but not its raison d'être. What Beaudout never mentions in these interviews is the internal conflict that drove him to the sea. The nightmares, the numbness, the general malaise he lived with every day. The building and outfitting of the raft (for a second time, mind you) was a triumph for all involved, but the cast-off was a tragedy when you consider what Henri was leaving behind. The consulate, the clergy, the army, even the SPCA had all told them it was a suicide mission, and either blind confidence or consuming indifference pulled Beaudout out to sea that May 24.

"To us, it was the most necessary trip in the world," Henri later said.

They tethered the raft to the *Promise* and started on their way. But they were soon in trouble, as the front of the 10-ton vessel was dragged down into the water. They had to stop to adjust their tow, pulling the front of *L'Égaré II* right up to the back of the trawler while keeping the rope taut, to reduce the potential drag. RoseMarie and others took pictures from the harbour. In their parting words to the reporters, the raftsmen joked that they hoped to land in England: "There are too many papers and forms to be filled out for French customs officials." It was a parting shot at French bureaucracy.

As they were leaving on the expedition, they were decidedly undersupplied — they had food enough for maybe 40 days with extreme rationing. Even the cigarettes were rationed, with only three cigarettes to last from that first Thursday to Sunday. The crew drew straws to see who would get to smoke that week, which Gaston won. Three of the four heavy smoking Frenchmen from the 1950s would have to do without tobacco for days at a time. It was a recipe for mutiny if there ever was one. As they passed Chebucto Head, they changed into quilted, nylon-blend suits, which would repel water and hopefully keep them warm. A northeastern wind was with them. As the *Promise* cut ties and *L'Égaré II* drifted into international waters, Marc retrieved a special package that had been hidden in the cabin prior to their departure. From out of the package came Puce and Guiton. Marc held them up to the radio and had the kittens mew as the first official transmission from the raft. The six of them would now be adrift on the North Atlantic for what they assumed would be 100 days.

L'Égaré II is tethered to the *Promise* to be towed out to sea, sometime after 4 p.m. on May 24, 1956.

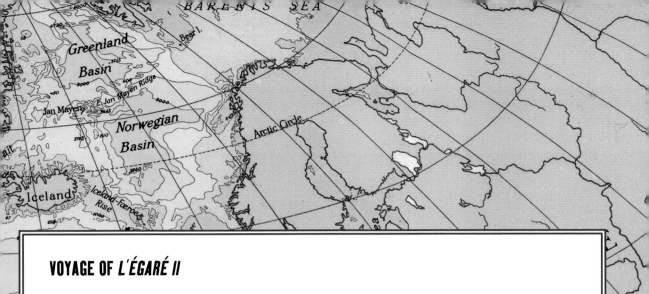

VOYAGE OF *L'ÉGARÉ II*

REBUILDING
March 1, 1956, to May 24, 1956

RAFT CONSTRUCTION
- Base: 9 metres (30 feet) long × 5 metres (17 feet) wide. Constructed of 9 base logs and 6 crossbars, all of British Columbia red cedar, held together by 1,800 metres (6,000 feet) of manila rope.
- Cabin: 1.2 metres (4 feet) high × 3 metres (10 feet) long × 2 metres (7 feet) wide. Constructed of laths of wood, basket woven by hand.
- Masts: 2; 7.6 metres (25 feet) long of local light wood, set in a V shape.
- Booms: 6; mobile booms, each 1.8 metres (6 feet) long and 0.3 metres (1 foot) wide assure the drift; one rudder in the shape of an oar, the direction.
- Sail: 1; 5.8 metres (19 feet) tall x 4.3 metres (14 feet) wide, made from Egyptian cotton.

RAFT STORES
- 50 kilograms (110 pounds) potatoes
- 4.5 kilograms (10 pounds) flour
- 17 sliced and toasted loaves of bread
- 40 cans of soup
- 10 jars of pickled pork tongues
- 3 cans of sausages
- 100 cans freshwater
- 15 kilograms (34 pounds) rice
- 4.5 kilograms (10 pounds) dried beans
- 70 small jars of meat paste
- 13 cans of corned beef
- 4 cans of pork loaf
- 50 cans of apple juice

CHAPTER 3
SiCK MAN ABOARD

"THERE APPEARED to be a link between United States coastguard radio reports [of a sea monster] and a Halifax marine radio message concerning the apparently unmanned raft drifting some 30 miles off Sable Island."

— *Chronicle Herald*, June 8, 1956

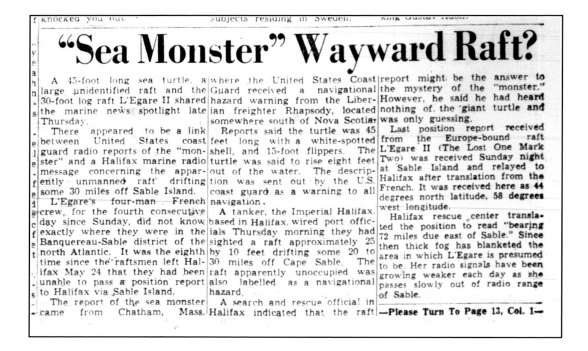

"Sea Monster" Wayward Raft?

A 45-foot long sea turtle, a large unidentified raft and the 30-foot log raft L'Egare II shared the marine news spotlight late Thursday.

There appeared to be a link between United States coast guard radio reports of the "monster" and a Halifax marine radio message concerning the apparently unmanned raft drifting some 30 miles off Sable Island.

L'Egare's four-man French crew, for the fourth consecutive day since Sunday, did not know exactly where they were in the Banquereau-Sable district of the north Atlantic. It was the eighth time since the raftsmen left Halifax May 24 that they had been unable to pass a position report to Halifax via Sable Island.

The report of the sea monster came from Chatham, Mass. where the United States Coast Guard received a navigational hazard warning from the Liberian freighter Rhapsody, located somewhere south of Nova Scotia.

Reports said the turtle was 45 feet long with a white-spotted shell, and 15-foot flippers. The turtle was said to rise eight feet out of the water. The description was sent out by the U.S. coast guard as a warning to all navigation.

A tanker, the Imperial Halifax, based in Halifax, wired port officials Thursday morning they had sighted a raft approximately 25 by 10 feet drifting some 20 to 30 miles off Cape Sable. The raft apparently unoccupied was also labelled as a navigational hazard.

A search and rescue official in Halifax indicated that the raft report might be the answer to the mystery of the "monster." However, he said he had heard nothing of the giant turtle and was only guessing.

Last position report received from the Europe-bound raft L'Egare II (The Lost One Mark Two) was received Sunday night at Sable Island and relayed to Halifax after translation from the French. It was received here as 44 degrees north latitude, 58 degrees west longitude.

Halifax rescue center translated the position to read "bearing 72 miles due east of Sable." Since then heavy fog has blanketed the area in which L'Egare is presumed to be. Her radio signals have been growing weaker each day as she passes slowly out of radio range of Sable.

—Please Turn To Page 13, Col. 1—

Halifax *Chronicle Herald*, June 8, 1956.

JUST WEEKS out to sea and nobody knew where to find *L'Égaré II*. The men had been sent adrift on the evening of May 24 and had only experienced seven sunny days in the first 20 of their voyage. The lack of sun made it colder and increasingly difficult for Henri to plot their position on a map. Persistent fog diminished visibility to sometimes less than 300 metres (1,000 feet). Ham radio operators had picked up *L'Égaré II*'s signals at Moncton, Stellarton and Dartmouth, but with a transmission reach of just 483 kilometres (300 miles), the raftsmen had been completely out of contact for days at a time.

By June 8, 1956, ten days had passed since Henri Beaudout had been able to accurately determine their location on a navigation chart. It's no wonder that Maritime radio networks began to receive confusing reports. That same day, a "sea monster" was spotted off the

Stormy skies on the North Atlantic.

coast of Nova Scotia. The Liberian freighter *Rhapsody* called the U.S. coast guard to inform them of a sea turtle 14 metres (45 feet) long. Also that day, the *Imperial Halifax,* a tanker out of Nova Scotia, reported seeing an unmanned raft drifting some 40 kilometres (25 miles) off Sable Island.

Their journey from Halifax toward the Gulf Stream was not dissimilar to the one that Henri and Gaston had experienced along the St. Lawrence a year earlier, when winds had been unfavourable from the beginning.

Upon departure, the crew had thought the wind and current would carry them across the vast ocean like some sort of express train. However, as tended to be the case for the crew of *L'Égaré II*, not all went as planned. Just four days into the voyage, they hit their first patch of bad weather. "Soon enough, it became clear that we were at the mercy of the wind and current," Marc Modena wrote. A storm with winds at 64 kilometres (40 miles) an hour had rocked the raft, sending the boys into the three-person cabin for refuge.

It was during this first storm that they started what would become their practice during severe weather: they tied themselves

Day 7

One week at sea and we've made almost no progress.

The wind is against us ...

... and the fog is thick as soup.

Sable Island is out there. I wonder if the others appreciate the danger.

together at the waist and then to the raft. "The raft was unsinkable," Henri later asserted. "As long as we stayed on the raft, we would be okay." But they weren't all okay. That first storm triggered what would become chronic seasickness for Jose Martinez — a sickness that would not be helped by the severe rationing the men were forced to follow.

On their first evening at sea, shortly after bidding adieu to Captain Henneberry and the *Promise*, Henri had Marc take stock of their stores. After a quick inventory and calculation, Modena estimated that they had food enough for 42 days.

"We weren't worried," Marc would later write in his self-published memoir, *L'argonaute*. "Optimism had us thinking, the ocean was full of fish, and we could catch those fish, compensating for our largely meager rations." Gaston even joked that they would be able to sell fish when they arrived in port, because they would never be able to eat it all.

However, being a prudent skipper, Beaudout immediately cut the crew's rations their first morning on the Atlantic. Each crew member received one cup of coffee, two pieces of bread, a bowl of soup, one potato and one pint of saltwater mixed with two pints of freshwater.

"We had been accustomed to privation from childhood," Beaudout wrote. "We had all learnt early in our lives how to suffer. We knew that the rations we were imposing on ourselves would weaken us physically, even at times, perhaps, cause us to be indisposed, but we knew that nothing could weaken us morally." He recalled this exchange:

"And when we have nothing further to eat, what happens then?" Marc asked of Henri.

"We then start on the ropes," he replied.

"*Bon!*" said Marc. "Then I shall start on the thickest, the ones that have been dragged through the water longest; they will be the juiciest."

RoseMarie Comeau followed the journey of *L'Égaré II* and the boys through newspaper coverage. Every day, she would check the Halifax *Chronicle Herald* for updates on her friends, which arrived via radio operator Aaron Solomon. When she found them, the secretary of the expedition dutifully snipped out the articles and put them in her scrapbook.

On the morning of June 1, she had opened the paper to find a headline that chilled her to the bone: "Raft Moving Eastward Towards Sable Island." Located in an area known as the "graveyard of the North Atlantic," Sable Island is about 300 kilometres (186 miles) southeast of

FACING PAGE: Marc counting rations the early evening of May 24th.

the Dartmouth Slip. This crescent-shaped landmass consists of sand dunes on its south side, which can run 12 metres (40 feet) high and are constantly shifting — a risk to passing ships. The waters of the north side are cold and fast moving, dotted with whirlpools. Well over 100 ships had foundered in the waters off these shores in the previous decades.

"I was worried because I knew how dangerous Sable Island was," Comeau recalled. "Coming from a small fishing community in Nova Scotia, I had heard stories of what could happen near Sable." Her own grandmother had lost four brothers in those very waters years earlier. She had warned Henri of this area — if they were to end

"We knew that the rations we were imposing on ourselves would weaken us physically ... but we knew that nothing could weaken us morally."
— Henri Beaudout

Lifelong Citizen Of Halifax Passes

Raft Moving Eastward Towards Sable Island

Four French adventurers aboard the 30-foot log raft L'Egare II reported to amateur radio operators of the Maritime phone net late Thursday they again did not know their exact position. They said they had seen Sable Island's east light about 10.15 p.m. Wednesday and figured they were "quite close to the east bar" of the graveyard of the North Atlantic.

Wednesday night Marc Modena, the raft's radioman, relayed their position as 28 miles south-south-west of Sable. For two days previous the raftsmen did not know just where they were. Absence of a visible sun prevented their shooting a sextant fix.

Search and rescue officials at Halifax said the raft appeared to be in no immediate danger.

The Frenchmen said late Thursday they were about northeast of Sable and drifting eastward. They inquired how far east they would

have to shift to clear the island's east bar. Maritime phone net operators told them 20 miles would do the trick.

The raft left Halifax a week ago on a drift-and-sail voyage to the European continental shelf. The "voyageurs" hope to make the long trip home in three months.

Weathermen said the Sable district was in for scattered showers late Thursday night, accompanied by southwesterly winds of about 15 miles an hour. Extensive fog patches were predicted for the area, some 180 miles southeast of Halifax.

Visibility was expected to be 10 miles, dropping to two miles in showers and near zero in fog, the weather office said. Temperatures would be mild.

Halifax Chronicle Herald, *June 1, 1956.*

up in the drink with *L'Égaré II* suffering the same fate as its predecessor, it would most likely be here.

Henri had hoped to sail around the south side of the island, a more direct route to the Gulf Stream, but as they approached, a thick fog descended over the water. Afraid of running ashore, the men dropped sail. All four stood lookout for any landmarks. They could hear waves crashing on the shore — that's how near they were — but still could see nothing. Then Gaston, stationed atop the cabin, spotted the light from the Sable Island lighthouse. As they feared, they were headed directly for the shore. A southwest wind prevented them from following their route, so Beaudout quickly decided to use the rudder to push the raft in the other direction, through the treacherous waters of the north side of the island.

Marc radioed ashore asking how far they should travel in their current bearing to avoid collision with the island. For every kilometre (5/8 mile) they journeyed north, they were 3 kilometres (nearly 2 miles) farther from their goal of reaching the Gulf Stream — precious distance lost for a vessel at the mercy of the elements. They had about 30 kilometres (19 miles) to go before they would be out of danger.

Temperatures on the North Atlantic in those early days of the trip hovered around 5.5°C (42°F). Conditions were made all the more uncomfortable by the inescapable moisture. Even the cabin was constantly wet, especially after that first storm. Jose later complained to reporters that there was "always water on the floor." He said it was very damp and their clothes were wet. Henri echoed these sentiments: "We felt so cold that it seemed we should never be warm again."

Both Henri and Marc self-published memoirs chronicling their time aboard *L'Égaré II*. Henri has also given interviews in later years, including several for this book. Gaston left behind his photographic record of the journey. But Jose Martinez left little trace of his time aboard the raft. He remains a mystery — a missing piece in the tale of *L'Égaré II*. For his story, we have had to glean plausible details from the accounts of the others, as well as the newspaper coverage from the time.

Henri and Marc both wrote of Jose's seasickness, which began almost immediately after their departure and was exacerbated by the storms the crew faced early on in their journey. "We noticed at once that Jose was the person who had suffered most from the long hours of rough weather," Beaudout recorded in his journals. "He had been very seasick, and this seemed to make a completely different man of him."

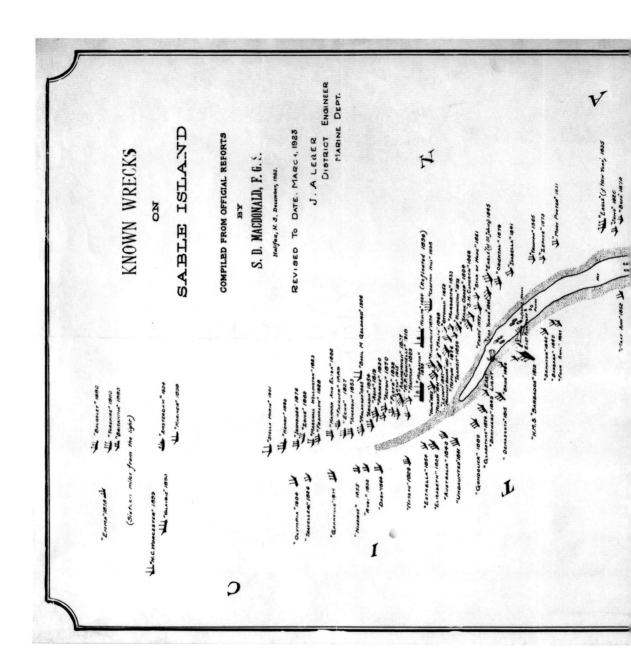

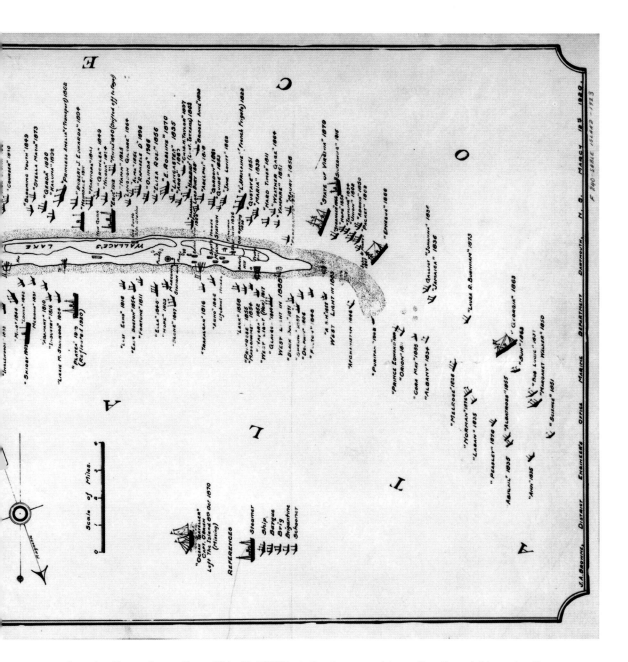

An updated issue of a map first published in 1882 illustrating the names, dates and locations of shipwrecks off the coast of Sable Island from 1802 to 1922. Vessels are identified as steamers, ships, barques, brigs, brigantines and schooners. Lighthouses, semaphore flags and Marconi stations are also shown.

In its first month at sea, the raft had managed to cover just a tenth of the distance from Halifax to Europe, and as time dragged on, Jose grew sicker. Both Modena and Beaudout wrote that their cook spent his days sitting on a box, staring off into a dream world. He eventually gave up his duties, no longer taking his two-hour watch at night or preparing the crew's meals.

Halifax *Chronicle Herald*, June 12, 1956.

Interestingly enough, at this very time, the Halifax *Chronicle Herald* published an article by Dr. Edwin P. Jordan entitled "Seasickness Makes You Want to Die." In it, Dr. Jordan describes seasickness from the point of view of the afflicted: "Usually, the victim has been feeling fine and in good spirits and suddenly becomes quiet and subdued," he writes. "He begins to feel nauseated and mentally depressed. Life no longer seems worth living."

Henri recalls seeing Jose kneeling on the deck of the raft, his forehead pressed against the logs for quite a long time. It wasn't long after their brush with Sable Island that Jose would go to Henri and ask to be transferred onto the next passing ship. That evening, Henri wrote in his log, "Jose is still ill. He is constipated and has developed a hatred of the sea. We watch out for a boat."

Day 13

Where is our cook?

Sleeping.

I took his breakfast duty.

He says he won't eat.

Can I have his ration?

Newspapers first reported of Jose's illness on June 12. "We have a sick man on board," the message from Marc was reported to go. "He would like to return to Canada." That message, transmitted on June 8, included no special rescue request — if Jose were to be saved, he would have to wait. And wait he did, for nearly two weeks.

During this time, the crew's rations were rapidly depleting. Their plan to supplement with fish they caught along the way hadn't worked out. In the cold waters of the North Atlantic, the fish remained deep below the surface, well out of reach of their fishing lines and the tridents each man had fashioned for himself. They fished in vain for weeks — all the while, their stores grew smaller and smaller, even with Jose often passing on his share.

The weather also continued to be unfavourable, as storms routinely tested the raft and the men. For Jose, it was a desperate and miserable situation with little sign of relief. Then disaster struck on day 19.

Marc inspecting a fishing net. Jose can be seen in the background.

Day 19

MARC! GET THAT SAIL DOWN BEFORE IT'S TORN TO RIBBONS!

WHOA!

WHAT THE HELL IS THAT?

Later

We lost 30 pounds of rice.

With current rations we've got food for 15 days.

I guess we'll cut the rations.

Who's got the energy to eat, anyway?

After losing the rice, rations were further cut to one potato and one piece of toast. The situation on board was untenable. To Beaudout, Jose Martinez needed to disembark and they needed to reach the Gulf Stream before the three remaining crew members starved to death.

Finally, on the evening of June 20, twelve days after deciding that Jose had to leave the expedition, Henri spotted the Canadian research vessel *Investigator II* off their starboard side. Henri fired a flare into the sky to catch the passing ship's attention. Captain William Barbour, the man in charge of *Investigator II,* lowered a long boat into the water to collect the ailing man.

"I assumed that we all had the same ideal in mind: the making of one sublime effort to accomplish something which might, and probably would, demand all we had to give," Henri later wrote. "I could not imagine any conditions defeating any of us morally … Jose Martinez must have conceived the expedition from an entirely different aspect. The physical weakness that overtook us all because of our rations and the cold and damp conditions was, apparently, too much for him."

Jose leaves the raft on June 20, 1956, 27 days into the voyage.

Speaking to reporters after his return to the mainland, Jose would say that he sought only an adventure. *The Daily News* out of St. John's, Newfoundland, published a two-page article covering his return. In the article, there is the briefest of excerpts from his own journals kept while aboard the raft. The article also reveals that, like Henri, Jose had a wife waiting for him. "I want to go back to Montreal as quickly as I can," he told reporters. He assumed his job was gone but hoped to get another one working with his father-in-law. "[He] makes pop," Jose explained. Upon his return, he would pay a visit to Mrs. Beaudout, letter from Henri in hand.

"Every day for the past few weeks, a young wife has been telephoning British United Press in Montreal to ask 'Any news of my husband?'"

In an article published around the time of Jose's return, a Montreal paper catches up with Jeannine Beaudout. Like RoseMarie, Henri's wife had been tracking the progress of her husband and his raft through news reports — that is, until *L'Égaré II* had progressed to the point where it was no longer in range to make regular, daily radio contact. "What does a wife do when her husband informs her he wants to cross the Atlantic on a raft measuring 30 feet by 17 feet?" the writer asks. "Pretty dark-eyed Mrs. Beaudout says she didn't take much notice at first ... 'Once I saw it was an obsession with him,' she says, 'there was nothing to do but encourage him.'"

The article, which appeared under the heading "Women in the News," presents a picture of Jeannine's long, lonely wait for Henri's return. She reportedly passes her days doing housework, raising Chantal and completing crossword puzzles. It ends as follows: "Young Mrs. Beaudout sits in her apartment by the St. Lawrence River. She looks at the map on the wall, twists her husband's wedding ring, which she wears under her own, and says cheerfully: 'There's no reason why they shouldn't make it.'"

Montreal, 1956

Chantal?

What are you doing?

Looking for Papa.

HALIFAX

SABLE iSLAND

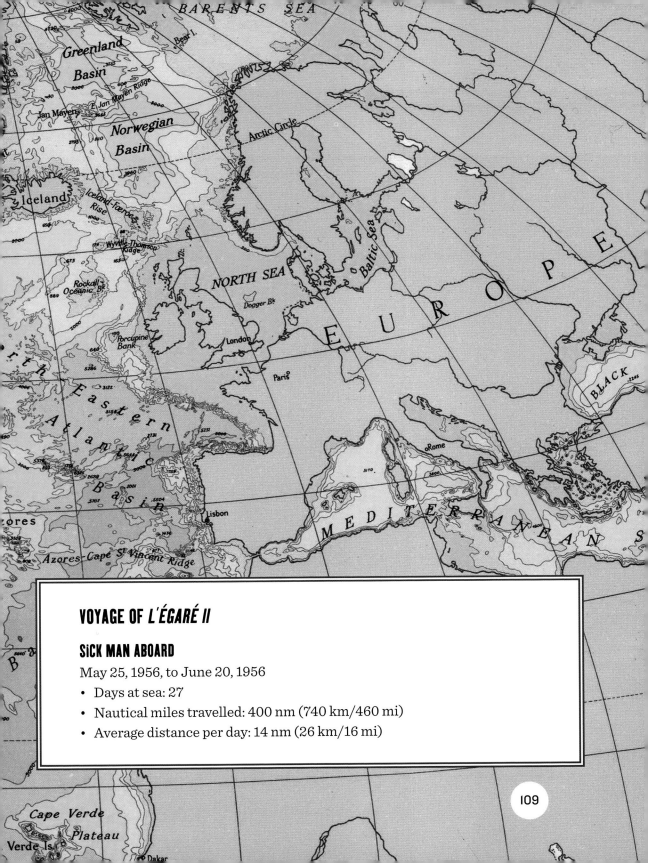

VOYAGE OF *L'ÉGARÉ II*

SICK MAN ABOARD

May 25, 1956, to June 20, 1956

- Days at sea: 27
- Nautical miles travelled: 400 nm (740 km/460 mi)
- Average distance per day: 14 nm (26 km/16 mi)

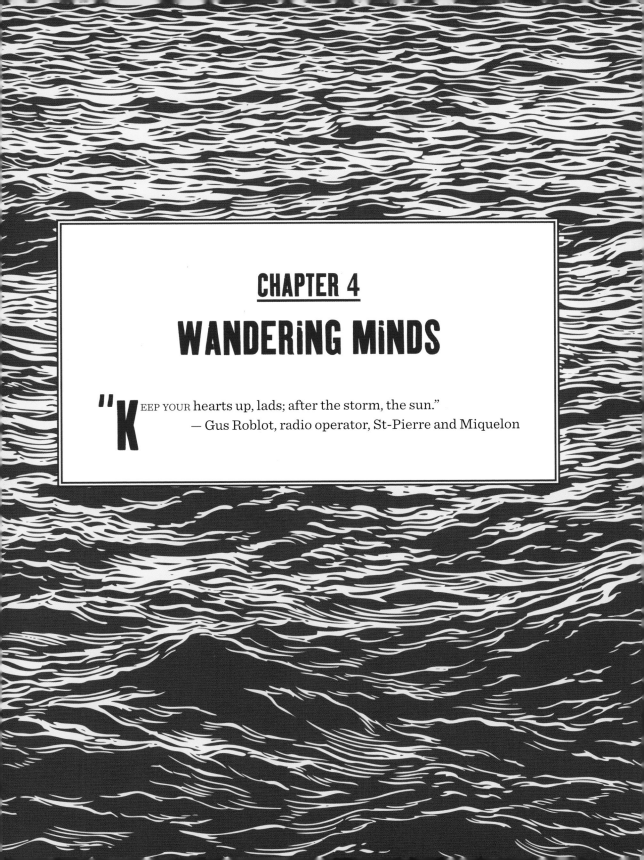

CHAPTER 4
WANDERiNG MiNDS

"KEEP YOUR hearts up, lads; after the storm, the sun."
— Gus Roblot, radio operator, St-Pierre and Miquelon

JUST AFTER the crew of *L'Égaré II* had been hammered by the biggest storm they had yet encountered on the open sea, they received that motivating message from radio operator Gus Roblot of St-Pierre and Miquelon. It was June 23, just three days since Jose Martinez had begun his journey back to the mainland.

"We can feel the raft lifting itself on the vast rollers, as if angry at this treatment," Henri wrote in his journal. "We can hear the waves as they pass under the logs crashing against the wood centreboards, causing them to vibrate. Any moment we expect them to be torn off."

As it turned out, the kittens served as reliable barometers for the sailors — a kind of early weather-warning system. If ever the men spotted the cats going into hiding in the raft's sleeping quarters,

Marc, left, and Henri, right, are tied to the cabin as they wait out a storm.

they knew to drop their square sail for fear of losing it and prepare to get wet. The three would tie themselves together and then to the raft, the system they had developed when waiting out the first storm. The thinking was, should one man be swept overboard due to rough weather, the others stood a chance of pulling him back on deck.

Marc making breakfast.

Henri Beaudout felt it a certainty that it was less dangerous to cross the Atlantic on his raft than in a sailboat. "Those logs were 1 ½ feet [45 centimetres] in diameter — the thickest was 2 feet [60 centimetres]. And at 30 feet [9 metres] long, we weren't talking matchsticks. They were sturdy. Even if we'd struck an iceberg, we'd have just ended up

collecting a bit of ice at the edge of the raft — enough for the cocktails we didn't have."

The storm on June 23 roared and raged, but amounted to nothing but wet clothes. The next day would be their 31st at sea — it was also St-Jean-Baptiste Day, the national holiday of their adopted province of Quebec. The raftsmen marked the occasion with a piece of toast and a large spoonful of beans. Hardly the champagne and *tarte au sucre* one might want to celebrate with, but it would do in a pinch. *L'Égaré II* had travelled some 840 kilometres (520 miles) in that first month, averaging 26 kilometres (16 miles) a day.

At their current rate of progress, they wouldn't arrive in Europe for another 137 days — just 68 days past due, according to Henri's initial 100-day estimate. Food was still the problem, as it had been from the start of the expedition. Thirty-two days had passed and the boys had yet to successfully catch a single fish, a fact that was so unbelievably depressing that it was reported in the papers back home.

"Physically we were tired," Henri remembered years later. "We suffered from constipation — we lacked food, that's for sure." Their legs trembled as they moved about the raft, from weakness brought on by hunger. A solid month living on little more than bread, cigarettes and salty drinking water was beginning to take its toll on each man. Their clothes were a looser fit than they had been upon departure. Their beards just barely hid how gaunt their cheeks had become. Losing Jose had certainly freed up some of the rations, but splitting next to nothing three ways instead of four made little impact on their daily caloric intake.

"We can feel the raft lifting itself on the vast rollers, as if angry at this treatment."
— Henri Beaudout

"We had suffered deprivation in our lives," Henri would later say. "Deprivation, I knew what it was. I was deprived of a lot of things."

When the Armistice of June 22, 1940, was signed between officials from Germany's Third Reich and the French Third Republic, Henri Beaudout was just 13 years old. His days up to that point had been relatively carefree, spent, for example, challenging friends to see who could hold their breath underwater the longest. At the outbreak of the war, his father and uncle had enlisted to fight against Hitler's forces, leaving Henri and his mother back at home in Limoges. Armistice sent droves of refugees fleeing from occupied northern France into the unoccupied southern "Free Zone," governed by the Régime de Vichy. Henri had seen the refugees on the roads. Limoges, the capital of the Limousin region, was also a destination for Jews fleeing from Alsace.

French forces had been decimated in the northern battle, and the Vichy government, led by Chief of State Philippe Petain, was little more than a puppet regime serving Germany. Life in the "Free Zone" was anything but free. Food shortages resulted in stringent state rationing. Policies dictated by Germany led to mismanagement and malnourishment on a mass scale in Vichy.

Henri, right, as a young teenager.

This time of uncertainty and privation took its toll on Henri's mother. He remembers her waiting each day for word from her husband. After a restless night's sleep, she would often sit on the side of Henri's bed, and in the guise of consoling her young son, say things like, "My poor boy, what will we become without your papa?"

"With my head on the pillow, I would listen," Henri wrote. "But her pain was equalled in my rage to see our soldiers, and their officers in front, flee from the approaching enemy." From an early age, the war was black and white for young Henri Beaudout: Germans were the enemy and they must be fought and defeated no matter what the cost. As a boy, he saw the effects of the occupation in the north — the creep of collaboration among his neighbours.

"Rationing was draconian. Some dark bread, rutabagas, Jerusalem artichokes, and meat that was meant to last a week but wouldn't make a meal." Henri remembers his neighbour prostituting herself for a bit of meat, a bottle of wine or some cigarettes from traders on the black market. "Food traders became kings."

Word came one day from his father: he had been injured and was convalescing in Pau, a French city not far from the Spanish boarder. He was soon to be discharged and would return home shortly thereafter.

The area where Henri's family lived became a hotbed for Resistance activity. What had started as passive resistance in 1940 in Vichy, with the distribution of literature against the governing powers, escalated as the war dragged on and occupation spread into the southern zone in 1942. The Maquis du Limousin, the first organized resistance to form in France, chose to dynamite a power plant near Ussel in the Corrèze district as its initial act of violent disruption. By the age of 17, Henri was working for the Resistance movement as an active fighter.

Marc surveys a snapped rope — damage sustained from a storm.

FACING PAGE: Henri, top right, as a young *maquisard.*

The morning after St-Jean-Baptiste Day, the boys had tried again to eat seaweed — Marc fried it up with a little butter — but they found the prevailing taste of iodine to be too much to handle. Sunday had passed and it was now Monday. They had long burned away their seemingly generous rations of appetite-suppressing, store-bought cigarettes. (And until the following Sunday, they had to hand roll their tobacco, a task none of them was particularly skilled at and was only made more difficult by the motion and moisture aboard the raft.)

Marc started his morning by dragging a fishing line alongside the raft — something they had done every day since departing from Halifax. Only this morning, Marc got a bite. On the end of his line, he had hooked a 4.5-kilogram (10-pound) cod, and this fish wasn't getting away.

BELOW: The raftsmen clean their first catch.

RIGHT: Henri unhooks a fish.

"I didn't believe my eyes," Marc wrote of his catch. According to the man himself, it wasn't just the first fish of the expedition; it was the first fish he had ever caught in his 29 years. "Who is the best? Hey boys, who is the best?" he whooped with joy. Gaston shot some film for their records. Henri, a consummate fisherman since childhood, took up a line in an attempt to capitalize on the apparently hungry fish below. He tried to replicate Marc's success for quite some time, but to no avail. He returned the line to the new cook, who caught a second cod almost immediately. It was clear that that particular day belonged to Marc. By noon, he had cooked up the fish for the crew and the two kittens — all five enjoyed their first bit of fresh meat in over a month.

They ate well that day, as Henri would use a bit of the cod to catch three black-backed gulls, which they then ate for dinner. In his log, Henri stated: "It has been a really good day. Now all we need is a slightly more favourable wind to get us on our way across the ocean, but for the moment we have a wind from the southeast that is getting up stronger and stronger."

The addition of fish and fowl to their diet had an immediate effect on all three men: their legs stopped trembling. But it also brought with it an unexpected side effect. That night and the next, each would have his sleep disrupted by unnerving dreams. Gaston dreamt that he was travelling along the Amazon, while Marc's dreams were more stressful. Henri remembers that it was "dangerous to touch" Marc while he was sleeping, as he would awake quite violently.

"[These dreams] were chiefly, though not exclusively, pictures from our earlier lives in most extraordinary detail," Henri wrote. "Instinctively we could glance back in our minds to the long horrors of Occupation and the dull struggle to find places for ourselves in the world that had washed up to our young feet when the tide of war and brutality had receded." Most nights, asleep in a bunk, Henri would revisit his war years.

Germany, 1945

Abend.

Guten Abend.

Ou Vin.

Vy-nne.

TOK

TOK TOK

SWISH

KLACK

NNGH!

HNNGHH!

....!

SSCHUNNK

It was the end of June, and for days, *L'Égaré II* had been fighting rain and fog. It was as though someone or something had decided that the boys needed an additional challenge to match their renewed strength. In Henri's writing from the time, he was hopeful that the weather might break. He was also wistful on recalling his daughter's birthday, which he'd be missing.

"We might have good weather at any moment now. I think of my little daughter, Chantal, who in a few hours will be three years old and I shall not be with her to light the three candles and see her blow them out. It is one of her joys to blow out my lighter at all times ..."

At 9:00 a.m. on July 3, Gaston woke the other two in a panic. The ropes anchoring the sail had snapped — the mast was unstable and at risk of breaking. It took all three of them to secure the sail. No sooner had they solved this than conditions worsened: winds picked up to 72 kilometres (45 miles) per hour, pitching the raft sideways. Henri writes of an 11-metre (35-foot) wave that threatened them, crashing just in front of their vessel. At times like this — at all times, really — they were at the mercy of the elements. They worked their drill, lowering the sail and binding themselves in the cabin. As they sat tied together in their tiny cover, all they could do was watch as water infiltrated every part of their living quarters. Rarely, if ever, had they been dry since saying goodbye to the *Promise*, but this tempest managed to soak *everything*: their maps, their beds, their quilted suits and, worst of all, their radio. *L'Égaré II* lost its only connection to the outside world. They were never more vulnerable to total disaster.

"We can hear the waves as they pass under the logs ... Any moment we expect them to be torn off."
— Henri Beaudout

FACING PAGE: Henri, left, and Marc, right, scramble to get the sail down during a storm.

St Catherines Pt
St George's
Island
The Narrows
George
St George's
Harbour
Town Cut Channel
Coney Is
Kindley
St David's
Island
Airfield
Fort Bell
Harrington
Castle
Nonsuch I.
Sound
Harbour
Tucker's Town
32° 20'
N.
Mangrove L.
Flatts
200m

Baffin
Bay
GREENLAND

Hudson Bay
60°

50°

A M E R I C A

Quebec

HALIFAX

Grand
Newfoundland
Banks
St Flemish Cap

New York

Georges Bank

Washington

Bermuda

Newfoundland Rise

N o r t h - W e s t e r n   A t l a n t i c   B a s i n

Nares
Deep
SARGASSO
SEA

M I D - A T L A N T I C

Cape Ve

Puerto Rico Trench

RIBBEAN SEA
Venezuelan
Basin
Colombian
Basin

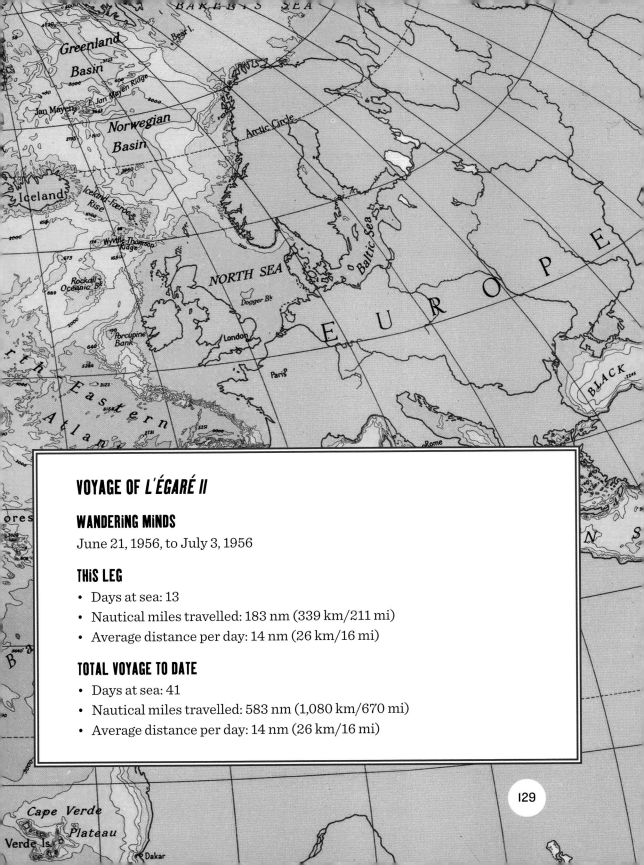

VOYAGE OF *L'ÉGARÉ II*

WANDERING MINDS
June 21, 1956, to July 3, 1956

THIS LEG
- Days at sea: 13
- Nautical miles travelled: 183 nm (339 km/211 mi)
- Average distance per day: 14 nm (26 km/16 mi)

TOTAL VOYAGE TO DATE
- Days at sea: 41
- Nautical miles travelled: 583 nm (1,080 km/670 mi)
- Average distance per day: 14 nm (26 km/16 mi)

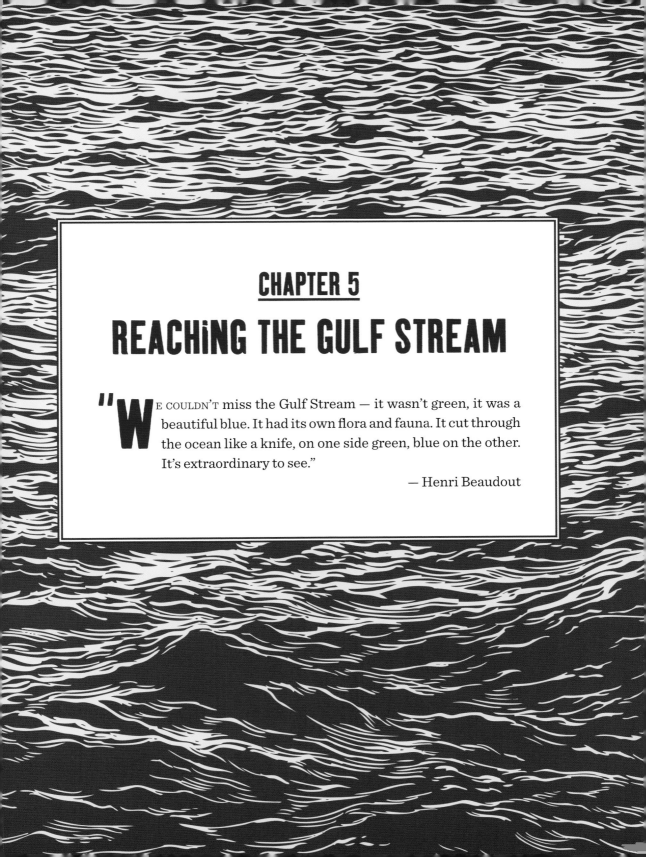

CHAPTER 5
REACHiNG THE GULF STREAM

"**W**E COULDN'T miss the Gulf Stream — it wasn't green, it was a beautiful blue. It had its own flora and fauna. It cut through the ocean like a knife, on one side green, blue on the other. It's extraordinary to see."

— Henri Beaudout

ASTON TOOK the temperature of the water three times — it had jumped from 2°C to 10°C (35.5°F to 50°F). The air had warmed enough that they could comfortably remove their outer layers. Photos and film footage show just how thin each man had become by this stage of the journey.

"I took off my trousers, but the sight of my sparrow legs caused me to get into them again," Henri wrote in his journal. "We certainly lost our youthful bloom blundering our way through the cold water and the fogs of the north."

The boys continued to pull off their damp layers — for the first time since departing Halifax, their clammy, wrinkled skin took in the bright afternoon sun. Even the cats seemed to recognize a marked difference in their circumstances and bounded about the sunlit deck of the raft.

The kittens, Puce (black) and Guiton (grey), play on the raft in the warmth of the Gulf Stream.

Ready?

Ready.

C'mere Guiton. It's warm in here.

TIK TIK

Hmm ...

Three knots.

Europe is a long way at three knots.

Henri, look ...

Sporting just their white undershirts, the men's arms were thin and ropey. Turning the crank to power the radio transmitter was now a two-man job.

Henri had spent weeks plotting their course and waiting for this day. He had watched helplessly as the raft was delayed, pushed off course and even had her progress reversed by unfavourable weather throughout the first leg of the journey. At various points along the way, his mind must have drifted to his and Gaston's time aboard the first *L'Égaré* and their constant battle with countervailing winds. *L'Égaré I* had been adrift for 70 days — nearly twice as long as their current journey by this point — and still had only managed to travel 1,300 kilometres (808 miles) before wrecking off the coast of Newfoundland. *L'Égaré II* was making better time than its ill-fated predecessor, but the crew knew they were still on a slower pace than what they'd envisioned for themselves.

"I'm not afraid to confirm, my friends, that this is a historic moment for us," Henri declared upon reaching the Gulf Stream. "We have entered the eternal *courant*, and the goal of our expedition." Thankfully, along with the warmer waters and air, their speed increased considerably. Henri estimated that they gained an additional 20 to 24 kilometres (12 to 15 miles) per day. For perhaps the first time in either *L'Égaré* expedition, the winds and waters were in their favour. They had taken an on-ramp to a highway across the North Atlantic. Although success was still a remote possibility, at the very least, this uptick in their speed of travel mitigated the chances of such disastrous outcomes as starvation and hypothermia. For now, they were in the warm embrace of the great North Atlantic Current — it was their best shot of reaching European shores before their stores dwindled to nothing and the winter air rolled over the North Atlantic.

"But, physically," Henri later wrote, "perhaps the greatest joy of the Gulf Stream was the fact that our feet were warm. They had never been less than frigid so far."

LEFT: Henri mans the tiller in his parka before entering the Gulf Stream.

RIGHT: Marc fashioning a trident tip in undershirt and shorts while in the warmth of the Gulf Stream.

Somewhere on the Atlantic ...

A view from the raft as it approaches a passing ship.

Upon entering the Gulf Stream, something else changed for the crew of *L'Égaré II:* more and more, they encountered passing ships in the North Atlantic.

The first such encounter was with a passenger ship. The U.S. naval ship *General R.E. Callan* spent World War II running troops from San Francisco to Honolulu. The ship was also one of three to rescue the crew of the U.S. Army transport *Joseph V. Connolly* when, in 1948, that ship burned up 1,600 kilometres (1,000 miles) out to sea from New York Harbor. Decommissioned for a time and manned by a civil service crew, the *Callan* was moving 340 military passengers across the North Atlantic to New York City when it came upon the raft and its crew in July 1956.

"The *Callan* is not a nice memory," Henri recalled years later. He had learned from St-Pierre and Miquelon radio operator Gus Roblot that the captain of the *Callan* had bragged about giving the boys food and that his charity had saved them from starving to death. It's a claim Henri calls "totally false."

The skipper of the *Callan* was Captain Harry D. Chemnitz. Looking at the available evidence, it does appear irrefutable that he did indeed give the boys food from his ship's stores. However, there are discrepancies between Chemnitz's account and those of Marc and Henri. The claim the raftsmen would have starved without the intervention may also have been a bit of good storytelling.

As reported in the newspapers of the day, the raftsmen put out a distress signal requesting medical assistance: "Their call was heard by the US naval transport *Callan* at 2:30 a.m. and, shortly afterwards, they got first aid." According to one newspaper, indigestion was the motivation behind the call for help. Another paper states that around 4:00 a.m., Chemnitz spotted an orange flare the raftsmen had fired off. However, neither Marc nor Henri mentions ever firing a distress signal in their written accounts. In fact, in Henri's log for the day, he writes of spotting a large ship coming straight for them, hoping he may be able to get some food for their stores. The encounter appears to be purely the result of chance.

The mast of *L'Égaré II* as it sits next to the *General R.E. Callan*.

According to the various accounts, Henri went aboard the *Callan* to speak with the captain. "Stammering in a heavy French accent, [Henri] said he could not speak English," one newspaper reported. "Captain Chemnitz, who does not speak French, sent a crewman to fetch his beret. 'I put on the beret,' the captain said, 'and that broke

MERRY MENAGERIE — By Walt Disney

"Well, after all, a tail is meant to be a flyswatter!"

Band Program For Wednesday

The band of the Royal Canadian Mounted Police Depot, under the direction of Inspector E. J. Lydall, will present the fifth concert in the Bandstand series in front of the Supreme Court Building, Wellington street, Wednesday evening, at 8.15, weather permitting.

The program:

[program listing]

Journal Want Ads bring quick results.

Bank of Canada Officer to Speak At Bankers' School

NEW BRUNSWICK, NJ, July 19 — (Special) — W. E. Scott, Bank of Canada research department chief, of Ottawa, will discuss the Canadian economy to world trade Wednesday at the ninth International Banking Summer School at Rutgers University here.

One of six other Canadian bankers attending the 11-day school is Robert J.P. Archambault of the Bank of Canada, 234 Wellington street, Ottawa.

The IBSS, meeting for the first time in the Western Hemisphere since founding in 1949 at Oxford University, is being attended by 300 bankers from 27 countries, including 18 from the USSR and its satellites. Sessions opened today.

ROAST DUCK DINNER FOR THREE ON RAFT

NEW YORK, July 18 — (P) — A Navy transport captain told yesterday how he gave help to three men on a raft drifting to Europe but had to don a beret to break down the language barrier.

The three men on the raft were French-Canadians, who said they left Halifax May 24 to sail the Gulf Stream to Europe.

Capt. Harry D. Chemta, skipper of the transport Gen. R. E. Callan which docked here, said the transport sighted an emergency orange flare at 4 a.m. Thursday about 1,000 miles east of Halifax.

The ship crew near, and found a log raft about 35 feet long and 25 feet wide with a cabin in the centre, a tiller, a large log sail, and three men aboard.

... a box on the raft bore the inscription "North Atlantic expedition" the raft was flying the flags of Canada, France, and the provinces of Ontario and Quebec.

Beret Broke Ice.

The raft sailed alongside the transport, and a mast wearing a beret with a large pompom clambered aboard the ship. Remembering in a beard Frenchman, he said he could not speak English.

Capt. Chemta, who does not speak French, said a sailor to fetch his beret.

"I put on the beret", the captain said, "and that broke the ice. I guess he figured I was one of them. From then on we understood one another perfectly."

It turned out that the raft skipper, Henri Beaumont of Montreal, spoke English fairly well but had been too nervous at first to find the right words.

Health Seemed Good.

Beaumont said he and his companions, Gaston Varsakteoe, a cameraman, and Marc Medina, a radioman, needed food because they had had no luck at fishing.

Chemta said he gave them fresh fruit, food staples and six roast ducks. They gave him seven pieces of mail, including letters to Mme Beaudoin in Montreal and Mme Vansakteoe in France.

A short time later the trio sailed off on their raft and the Callan proceeded to New York. A medical officer aboard the transport said the three men on the raft seemed to be in good health.

FREE FRANKS.

LONDON — (P) — American agricultural authorities will give away 250,000 hot dogs at their stand in the British food fair here in August.

---

see, hear, prove

the new **ZENITH** 10-in-1

eyeglass hearing aid

the amazing new **Crest**

- Wear it as an eyeglass hearing aid—or any number of other ways!
- At least twice the power of the average eyeglass aid!
- 10-Day Money-Back guarantee. Other Zenith aids from $50 to $150

COME IN TODAY!

PRIDHAM'S

"Authorized Zenith Hearing Aid Dealer"

182 Bank St., Room 705
CE3-1428

140-MILE WIND couldn't blow them off!

SELF-SEALING

Johns-Manville Seal-O-Matic ASPHALT SHINGLES

SEE YOUR NEAREST J-M DEALER

Ottawa and District Dealers

Carleton Insulating

Company Registered
FREE ESTIMATES

114 Sherbrooke St.   Phone 8-4304

M. N. Cummings Ltd.

Authorized Johns-Manville Dealer

382 Churchill St., cor. Scott   Phone PA2-3472

Thurso Lumber and Planing Mills

Company Limited

Thurso, Que.   District "J-M" Supplier   Phone 49

Insured Time Payment Plan

At Veitch-Draper our Time Payment Plan provides Life Insurance Protection for the person making the arrangements.

Veitch-Draper Ltd.

TRADITIONALLY FINE FUNERALS
PARKDALE AVE. AT GLADSTONE

T. Eldon Veitch   Kenneth V. Draper

the ice. I guess he figured I was one of them. From then on we understood one another perfectly.'"

Chemnitz claims to have given Henri fresh fruit, food staples like sacks of flour and six roast ducks. He also agreed to take letters back to the mainland and mail them to Jeannine in Montreal, and to the families of Marc and Gaston in France. Henri, in his own journals, writes of the *Callan* giving them enough food to last three weeks — certainly, it appears that Chemnitz's account is true. But it is likely that Henri objected to the tone of the coverage, including the *Ottawa Journal* headline: "Roast Duck Dinner for Three on Raft."

The *General R.E. Callan* as it departs *L'Égaré II*.

FACING PAGE: The offending headline and article from the July 10, 1956, issue of the *Ottawa Journal*.

The *Callan* may have provided the crew of *L'Égaré II* with additional stores, but they certainly weren't feasting, as that headline suggested. For one thing, the ducks the *Callan* supplied didn't come with thighs. "Curious beasts," Gaston said when he saw the legless fowl.

Captain Chemnitz was also no doubt a bit of a showman. At the time, Henri wrote of his fellow skipper: "The Captain had been very interested in our enterprise, the progress we had made and the stores on which we had subsisted." Henri had wanted to pay him for the ad-

SIGHT OF BERET LOOSENS TONGUE AND ENDS RAFT'S CRISIS AT SEA.
— *St. Louis Post-Dispatch*, July 10, 1956

dition to their stores, but reportedly his offer of Canadian currency was laughed off. Chemnitz wasted no time in relaying his story to the papers on the same day he reached port in New York City.

Missing from Chemnitz's account, but common in both those of Marc and Henri, is the danger the *Callan* posed to the petite *L'Égaré II* as the two vessels parted ways. The ship sat above the water, Marc remembered, with a quarter-diameter of its great propeller breaching the surface. As the ship powered on toward New York, it nearly sucked the raft into its propeller. "Twice we had to call to her to stop her engines," Henri later wrote, "and it was with the greatest exercise of our amateur seamanship that we got clear of her — even then not without suffering a broken cross-tree to our mast."

Not one account from this time speaks of Roblot contacting *L'Égaré II* with news of Chemnitz's story to the papers. Moreover, Henri's journal entries printed in the September 1956 issue of *Paris Match* and his subsequent book on their journey recount the meeting with the *Callan* in more or less the same detail as Chemnitz's version. However, in 1961, a 62-minute travelogue on the voyage of *L'Égaré II* was released. In this film, entitled *Atlantic Adventure*, there is no mention of the *Callan* — it is as though the encounter never happened. It stands to reason that sometime between 1957 and 1961, Henri Beaudout discovered Captain Chemnitz's press coverage and decided

to write him out of the official story. To Henri, and perhaps to Marc as well (who only devoted a dozen lines to the fateful encounter in his own memoir), Captain Chemnitz and the *General R.E. Callan* were not integral to the success of their voyage. Though his food certainly did make things easier for the three on the raft, there's little doubt the men felt they could survive on their limited rations and what they could catch. As they'd joked during the storms that marked the early days of their expedition, when pushed to the limit, they'd eat the ropes if necessary.

In the days that followed, the crew encountered more ships travelling through the Gulf Stream, including the USS *General W.C. Langfitt*. In his journals, Henri writes of being embarrassed when encountering these ships. He and the other crew members were self-conscious about their physical condition in front of these hearty sailors at sea. Henri writes that he, Marc and Gaston attempted to appear more substantial than they were at the time — more meaty.

Each time they encountered another ship, they faced the same danger of being sucked into her propeller upon departure. They began to loathe seeing another vessel on the horizon. One morning, Henri awoke to the sound of an engine. When he poked his head outside the cabin door, he saw a German cargo ship practically touching the raft. The German captain believed that he had stumbled upon survivors of a shipwreck and attempted to bring the boys aboard. They declined the offer but asked the captain for their current coordinates. That was Saturday, July 7, 1956. The next day, the barometer would drop and the kittens would go into hiding — the raft was about to experience more rough weather at sea.

Marc, Puce and Guiton look out at the sun setting over the Atlantic.

St George's
Island
St Catherines Pt
The Narrows
St George
Town Cut Channel
St David's
Island
Coney Is
Kindley
Air-field
Fort Bell
Nonsuch I.
y's Bays
Castle
Harbour
32° 20'
N.
Tucker's Town
Harrington
Sound
Mangrove L.
The Flatts
Bay
200m

Baffin
Bay

GREENLA

Hudson Bay

60°

Davis Strait

Baffin-Green
land Rises

3000

4326

AMERICA

50°

St Flemish Cap

Quebec

HALIFAX

Grand
Newfoundland
Banks

Basin

New York

Sable

5120

Washington

Georges Bank

5198

Newfoundland Rise

Mud Seamount

6491

6309

1553

5285

Western

Atlantic

Bermuda

Nares

Deep

North

SARGASSO
SEA

Mid-Atlantic

Puerto Rico Trench

Cape Ve

146

Venezuelan
Basin

Rise

RIBBEAN SEA

Colombian

MID ATLANTIC

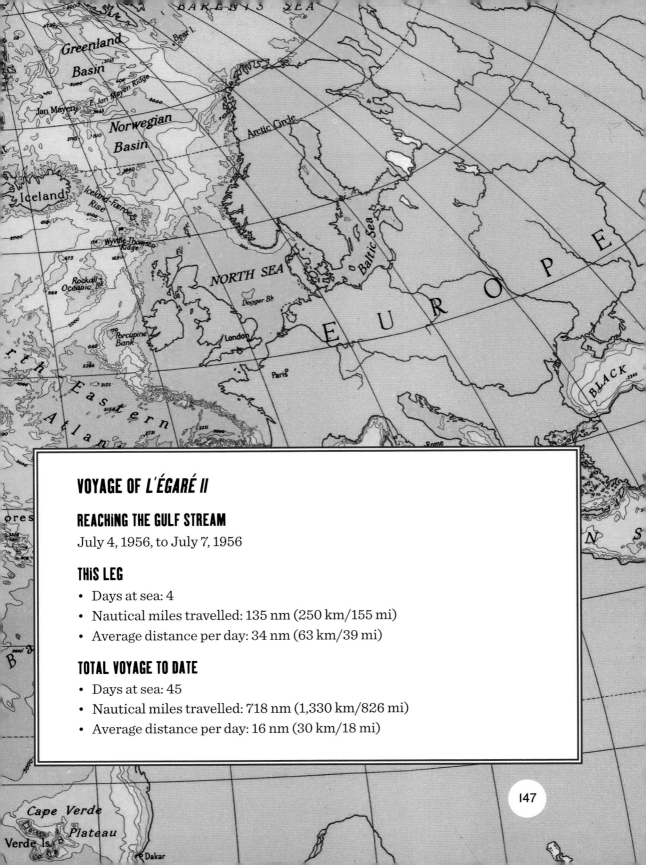

VOYAGE OF *L'ÉGARÉ II*

REACHING THE GULF STREAM

July 4, 1956, to July 7, 1956

THIS LEG

- Days at sea: 4
- Nautical miles travelled: 135 nm (250 km/155 mi)
- Average distance per day: 34 nm (63 km/39 mi)

TOTAL VOYAGE TO DATE

- Days at sea: 45
- Nautical miles travelled: 718 nm (1,330 km/826 mi)
- Average distance per day: 16 nm (30 km/18 mi)

CHAPTER 6
LAST STRETCH

"THE SEA is raging, and the wind is growing more violent ... The sky is full of big, black clouds. Our skiff is shaken and tossed like a nutshell ... The cabin cracks in every corner. We are not going to close our eyes tonight."

— Log, *L'Égaré II*, July 8, 1956

N THE evening hours of Sunday, July 8, the crew of *L'Égaré II* saw the beginning of the most violent storm they had yet encountered on the North Atlantic. Winds at 72 kilometres (45 miles) per hour rocked the raft for hours as the boys clung to each other through the night. By 10:00 p.m. on Monday, conditions had not improved. The ocean had grown so violent that each man had to take turns holding the tiller against the swelling waters. In three-hour shifts, each one stood in the wind and driving rains, holding the tiller straight so as not to have the raft knocked off its course. Every rogue wave was like a blow to the chest.

Waves from a powerful storm swamp the raft.

The storm would go on hammering them for days, until it finally let up on July 12. As the rain stopped and the clouds parted, the boys were free to survey the damage. They discovered that one of their keel boards had been snapped by the waves. Henri and Marc considered fixing the board, which was designed to help the buoyant raft cut through the water. Without it, they would have trouble keeping the raft on course. However, the keel was located on the underside; one of them would have to go into the water, and under the raft, to replace it — an impossibility, even for this brave lot. With no other option, they decided instead to discard the broken keel and take their chances without it. They tossed the splintered lumber into the water and watched it float away.

Reaching the Gulf Stream had a strange effect on the crew. The weather was warm, they travelled at a reliable speed and there was peace in the radio silence. But the relative comfort of the North Atlantic Drift brought with it a pervading boredom. It could be dull at sea, day in and day out.

"It's time we arrived," Henri wrote in his log. Growing impatient, the crew had been estimating the raft's speed by tossing a ball of paper into the water and timing how long

Henri (standing) and Marc inspect a damaged keel board.

it took the vessel to pass it. "We do not know what to do with ourselves. No more newspapers or books to read. We've used them all up in calculating our speed. Our only distraction: cats. We play with them and spend most of our time exchanging ideas about everyday life."

They eventually fashioned a checkers set, which held a passing appeal. They also filled their time performing in front of the camera for Gaston. Henri had tasked Gaston with capturing a record of their journey. Gaston would be what film theorist André Bazin called the

Marc, left, and Henri, right, play checkers while Guiton looks on.

Marc feeds Puce and Guiton.

"cinematographic witness," attempting to capture the events of the voyage while still being a part of them. However, because Gaston was one in a crew of just three, capturing as-it-happened documentary footage of every moment was near impossible. As Bazin notes in his writing on the *Kon-Tiki* documentary (fittingly enough), "whenever something of significance occurred, the onset of a storm, for example, the crew were too busy to bother about running a camera." The same held true for the crew of *L'Égaré II*. If Gaston was needed to hold the rigging before their sail was torn to shreds, his filming took a back

Gaston, left, and Henri, right, relax in the relative comfort afforded by the Gulf Stream.

seat. So, when they had down time, the men would recreate the "highlights." You can see this clearly in the footage. In one scene, the men have their game of checkers disrupted by a sound, and they rush out of the cabin to find their sail flapping in the wind. They must wrestle it back under control. In another scene, Marc hauls a cod out of the water, and it flops about on the end of his homemade trident; a closer look reveals that by rolling his wrist, Marc is puppeteering a performance out of a fish that was likely caught minutes before off camera.

During this period, Henri wrote, "We have a lot of trouble keeping the logbook up to date, unable to remember what happened the minute before."

The men spent the days speculating about where they might land in Europe and what they might do there. Marc said that he hoped they would reach Ireland. Henri agreed: "The Irish are good humoured, sympathetic people. And they would ply us with heavy cream. Ireland is full of cows, y' know."

"And it's all just one big green field, without end. You can just lie down in the grass and watch the clouds in the sky. It'll be super," added Gaston.

"And Irish girls are just so sweet, they have little speckles of sunshine on their skin. I dream of catching a nice tan under those freckles," Marc said with a grin.

At night, their dreams continued to disrupt their sleep. One morning, Gaston recounted to the other men his dream from the previous night. He had been sitting on the deck of the raft, fishing, in the middle of a violent squall. He saw a huge wall of cresting waves that appeared to be made up of open envelopes, like the kind you would use to send a letter. Gaston pleaded with Henri to lower the sail before the mast was snapped in two. Henri laughed in his face, saying, "The whole point of my scientific experiment is to prove that waves cannot break this mast." "You're insane," Gaston responded, which sent Henri into a fit of laughter.

Reaching the Gulf Stream had a strange effect on the crew ... the relative comfort of the North Atlantic Drift brought with it a pervading boredom.

When Gaston awoke from the dream, he stepped outside the cabin to check the conditions of the Atlantic and reacquaint himself with reality. He was embarrassed by how thoroughly his own dream had confused his perception. And, as can happen from time to time, he had trouble shaking the residual resentment he had felt toward Henri in that moment.

A shark circles
L'Égaré II.

July 14 was the 167th Bastille Day. Parisians celebrated by watching the Algerian cavalry ride in formation down the Champs Élysées, as part of the annual parade. On the raft, the boys rang in the day with a cup of hot chocolate, a rare luxury indeed. Somewhere along the way that morning, they'd picked up an escort. Not far in the distance, a pod of porpoises followed alongside *L'Égaré II* for several kilometres.

Life in the Gulf Stream included daily contact with a wide variety of sea life, along with the passing ships. At any given time, hundreds of tiny fish would be following underneath the wooden raft. As *L'Égaré II* slipped through these warm waters, it collected seaweed and algae, and with that plant life came all sorts of creatures: "Small shells, camouflaged, and shoals of fish created a whole society in the shadow of our raft," Marc recalled. The men would periodically try harpooning some of the fish surrounding them, with decidedly mixed results. Marc continued his streak as the best fisherman among the group, if only because none of the others seemed to have had any luck in landing much more than bait. This micro-ecosystem beneath them did, however, have its drawbacks: where there is bait there are predators.

N 49 31, W 24 15
July 29, 1956

Hey!

I was winning —

Winning my eye!

SHARK, BOYS!

RATTLE
RATTLE

GASTON!

YOU'RE MAD!

Much better shot from the water! I'm going to film you snagging it!

And if he snags you first?

I'd count on you guys to film it!

SPARE CAMERA'S ON THE DECK!

Good ol' Gaston.

3 O'CLOCK, MEN!

The boys attempted to eat the shark after landing it, but it proved inedible, even in their increasingly hungry state. With rations diminishing with each passing day, and a new cold streak when it came to fishing, Marc announced that he would once again have to cut each sailor's rations. Up to that point, rations had already been severe — on one particular day, Marc gave each man a slice of toast, a bit of corned beef, a mouthful of spaghetti and a coffee, and this was intended as a "treat" following a particularly gruelling encounter with some bad weather.

"What are we training for, a Grand Prix, or what? We're not jockeys, you know," said Gaston.

Conditions were foggy in the first week of August, leaving Henri struggling to plot their position on his charts. The crew grew increasingly dependent on passing ships to confirm their location. These ships often made contact, understandably assuming that they had come across some sort of S.O.S. situation. Despite their broken communication, the boys were always quick to clear up the misunderstanding with the various British, American, Dutch or Scandinavian crews.

"We had become such egotists," Henri wrote in his log, "that we did not want anyone to share with us this life that we had chosen, which we alone were living in this atmosphere of rain and fog and storm, in which everything — even the prospect of continued existence — depended on the wayward moods of the wind."

"We had become such egotists that we did not want anyone to share with us this life that we had chosen, which we alone were living ... "
— Henri Beaudout

August 8 was a quiet night; the ocean air was still. Henri went over his charts before bed, analyzing their progress up to that point.

According to his calculations, they had covered 3,540 kilometres (2,200 miles) in just 77 days. With their work done for the day, he and Marc then retired for the night, leaving Gaston on watch.

A few hours later, Gaston burst into the cabin. He had just spotted a ship coming straight for them off their starboard side. Through the darkness, just a short distance away, they could see the green and red navigation lights — it was clear that whoever was piloting this ship hadn't seen them.

"Jesus Christ, he's going to cut us in half," Henri said. He climbed atop their cabin and began shouting and waving a lantern over his head. At the last second, the oncoming ship increased her speed, just in time to narrowly avoid crashing into the drifting raft. The resulting waves washed over *L'Égaré II*'s deck — the ship had narrowly missed them by just 18 metres (60 feet).

Marc climbs the mast to position himself as lookout.

FACING PAGE: Marc, right, and Henri, left, make doughnuts at a time of calm on the raft.

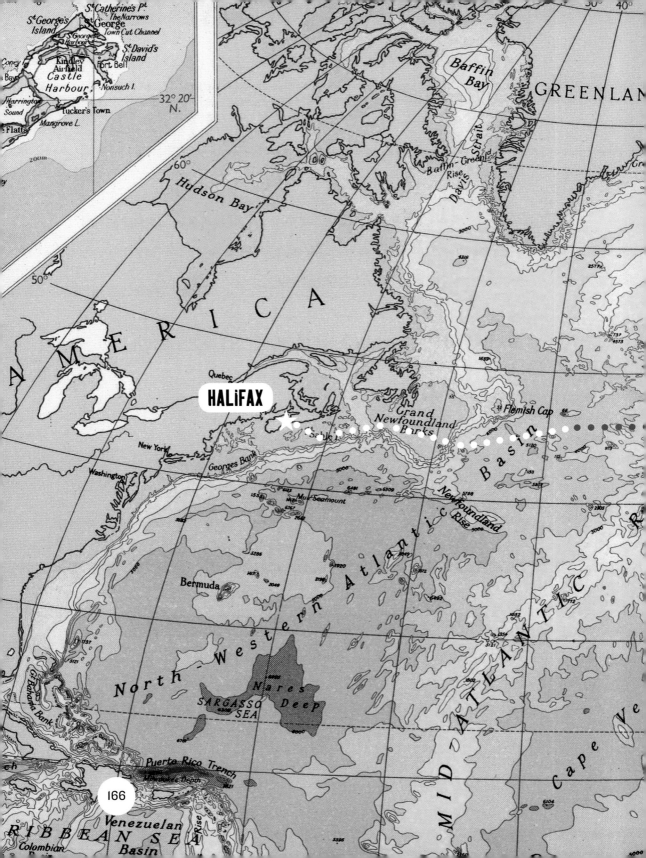

St Catherine's Pt
St George
St George's
Island
St George's Harbour
Town Cut Channel
St David's
Island
Kindley
Air field
Fort Bell
Coney I
Castle
Harbour
Nonsuch I.
Harrington
Sound
Tucker's Town
Mangrove L.
St Flatts
200m.
32° 20'
N.

Baffin
Bay

GREENLAN

Hudson Bay

Davis Strait

Baffin-Green

Rise

3000

5116

257

60°

50°

A M E R I C A

Quebec

HALIFAX

Grand
Newfoundland
Banks

St Flemish Cap
66

Basin

New York

Sable I.

Newfoundland
Rise

120

153

5505

Georges Bank

5000

6481

6309

5798

5801

Washington

1558

5761

768

Mur Seamount

5920

2205

3000

5286

1413

2049

1750

5712

Bermuda

5293

5852

Nares
Deep

SARGASSO
SEA

63088

6004

6000

4000

North-Western Atlantic

5121

6737

Gr Bahama Bank

5121

M I D - A T L A N T I C   R

Cape Ve

Puerto Rico Trench

Milwaukee Depth

8821

166

6104

Venezuelan
Rise

5395

RIBBEAN SEA
Colombian
Basin

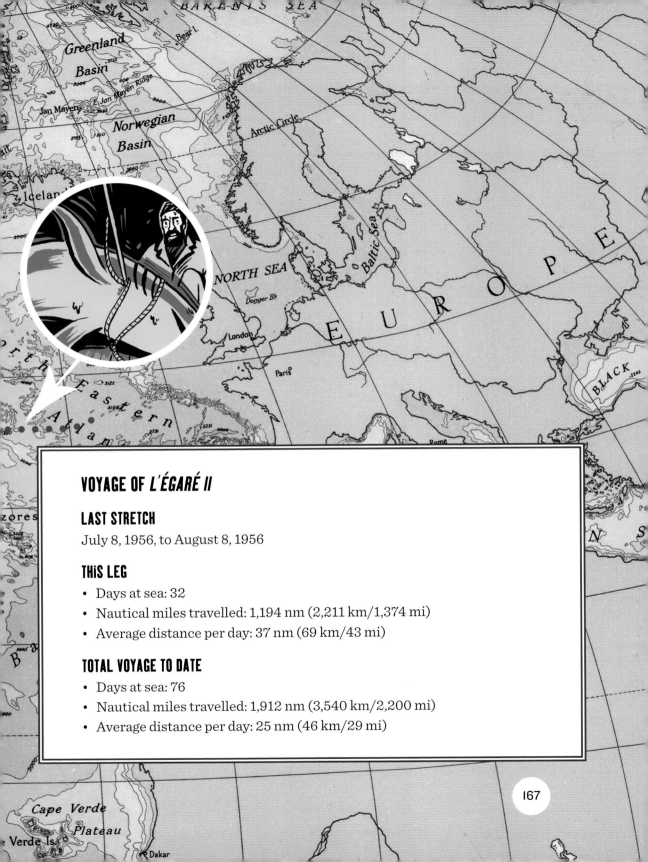

VOYAGE OF *L'ÉGARÉ II*

LAST STRETCH

July 8, 1956, to August 8, 1956

THIS LEG

- Days at sea: 32
- Nautical miles travelled: 1,194 nm (2,211 km/1,374 mi)
- Average distance per day: 37 nm (69 km/43 mi)

TOTAL VOYAGE TO DATE

- Days at sea: 76
- Nautical miles travelled: 1,912 nm (3,540 km/2,200 mi)
- Average distance per day: 25 nm (46 km/29 mi)

CHAPTER 7

ARRiVAL iN FALMOUTH

"ALREADY WE exchange ideas about what lies ahead ... What shall I do with my life? I do not want to return to the hydro company, planning electric circuits; I want to organize explorers' clubs and make people excited over the idea of adventure."

— Henri Beaudout

Dinnertime, August 19, 1956

A moment of silence for our last tin of beans.

It's time. We've got to be close.

I'm sure we'll see land any minute now ...

4 a.m., August 20, 1956

Now ...
NOW ...
NOW!

FIIIZZZZZZZZ

LAND HO!

Later

One of you come to shore with us. You'll need to clear some paperwork before you can dock.

Falmouth Harbour, England,
August 21, 1956

Well done, crazy French boys!

THEY HAD BEEN scrutinizing the horizon for days — while on watch, during their routine games of checkers, while Marc made their meals — and they knew they were close to land. The crew of *L'Égaré II* had been at sea for nearly three months, and by Henri's calculations, they appeared to be well ahead of their 100-day estimated schedule.

"We were searching for a sign, a signal, something to say, 'here is the land you're looking for,'" Marc recalled. "We decided to make a game of it and agreed that the first to cry 'land!' would get a glass of port." When Henri was the first to spot the lighthouse at Lizard Point, in the wee hours of Sunday morning, Marc quickly reminded his skipper that he had earned that glass of wine.

"I think it was one of the most intense moments of my life. When I saw England rise up out of the ocean just like that, at sunrise one morning, it was an extraordinary shock," Henri recalled. "An extraordinary moment that is utterly indescribable. I've never found the words to describe that moment."

In the excitement of that instant, Henri whooped and hollered — he was overjoyed, just as he had been when their raft reached the Gulf Stream. The end of this mad journey was finally in sight. Later that morning, *L'Égaré II* encountered the Dutch ship *Blyndyk* out of Rotterdam. *Blyndyk*'s captain offered to tow the boys to shore, but, aware it would delay the journey of this passing ship by several hours, Henri politely declined the offer. Before they parted ways, the captain confirmed that they were situated just off the Cornish coast, on course for Falmouth Harbour. He then radioed to shore to request a tow for *L'Égaré II*.

It wouldn't be long before the lifeboat from the village of Lizard reached them. However, there had been a misunderstanding: the

> **When I saw England rise up out of the ocean just like that, at sunrise one morning, it was an extraordinary shock."**
> **— Henri Beaudout**

174   The Raftsmen

lifeboat had come prepared for a rescue, not to tow several tons of timber. In fact, the skiff was far too small to pull the 10-ton *L'Égaré II*, even if it wanted to. The men of Lizard offered to take Henri ashore, where he could make his own arrangements for a tow into harbour. Reluctant to abandon his raft and its crew, Henri climbed aboard the other vessel and headed into the mainland — it had been 88 days since he last stood on solid ground. When he arrived ashore, he was immediately taken into custody.

"I was a French subject who had immigrated to Canada and had entered England from a raft without the necessary permits. Inquiries had to be made," Henri later wrote. After a period of questioning by mostly bemused immigration officials, Henri was offered a meal, but he refused, preferring to return to his friends on the raft and put a button on their journey across the North Atlantic.

By seven o'clock that evening, Henri had rejoined Marc and Gaston; the next day the three were then towed into Falmouth Harbour and greeted as conquering heroes. It was August 21, a full 89 days since their first morning adrift on the Atlantic. They had travelled some 4,700 kilometres (2,920 miles) powered only by wind and current.

"When we came into port," said Henri, "there were many boats ... boats of all sizes from all over the world and they all sounded their horns in salute. It was very emotional." The ships in port were coming at them in such numbers that Marc likened them to raindrops. Royal Air Force planes flew overhead, as the people of Falmouth gathered at the harbour to be the first to see the raftsmen after their successful transatlantic crossing. Henri was the most demonstrative among them, embracing both Gaston and Marc.

"We stood silently, overwhelmed by the emotion," Marc remembered. "The planes, the sirens, the warmth of this improvised reception: we were stupefied, vaguely intimidated, but profoundly happy."

For their part, Puce and Guiton were utterly terrified by the cacophonous greeting — they had grown accustomed to the relative peace

FACING PAGE:
Marc Modena climbs
to the dry land of
Falmouth Harbour on
August 21, 1956.

of sea life. They knew little more than the sounds of the ocean and the voices of the three raftsmen, and certainly nothing of throngs of shouting spectators or foghorns. But it would be some time before the kittens could greet the bulk of their well-wishers up close. As the three sailors went ashore, their mascots — their barometers, their confidantes — couldn't touch English soil; they were earmarked for quarantine.

The kittens, however, soon found new company on the raft. As one paper wrote: "Children, unhampered by police, swung from rope ladders and crawled like nautical ants over the rigging of the *L'Égaré II* while her owners began hectic negotiations with newspapers interested in their story rights."

After so long at sea, there were some aspects of living on dry land that the boys had to acclimate themselves to. For instance, they had earned their sea legs in that time. The muscles in their legs and backs had been working overtime to keep their equilibrium while aboard the raft as it bobbed, swayed and pitched continuously across the surface of the ocean. "The first time we stepped on land," Henri recalled, "the muscles were still moving, but the ground wasn't. So we walked like drunks. For quite some time, we looked like drunks."

In the end, they hadn't landed in Ireland, as Marc had once dreamed. Nor had they landed in Mr. Paterson's beloved Scottish homeland — they had landed in Cornwall. But the reception was well beyond anything they could have ever anticipated. The Cornish people welcomed Henri, Marc and Gaston with great enthusiasm. They were taken at once into the sailors' hostel and given a full English breakfast — eggs, bacon, toast,

"The planes, the sirens, the warmth of this improvised reception: we were stupefied, vaguely intimidated, but profoundly happy."
— Marc Modena

tomatoes, tea. They were shielded from the press as they regrouped. Henri had the opportunity to send a cable back home to Montreal and tell Jeannine that, in the end, he had been successful and that the three of them had arrived in England alive.

Henri washing off the salt of the Atlantic.

"The first thing we did was wash," Henri recalled. "Once we'd arrived, I remember I took three baths. I scrubbed myself, and each time I ran my hand over my skin, just as much dirt came off."

Once cleaned up and fed, they prepared themselves to meet with the newspapermen who were clamouring for their story. They sat behind a long table and steeled themselves for the negotiation. Before opening the doors, the patron of the boathouse turned to Henri and said: "Remember, the tables have turned." It took a second for the message to sink in, but Henri understood. For years now, he had been trying to convince people of his vision. Nobody much believed in him when he, along with three other men, mounted the first *L'Égaré*. And even those who did sure as hell stopped believing in this dream when that expedition ended in disaster. Henri and the others had been the subject of ridicule in the papers. And now, after they had succeeded in what they had set out to do, the news outlets were vying for the story — *their* story. Henri would have just this one chance to make them pay for it — for the story, and everything else.

When the doors were opened, it was chaos, with journalists scrambling to get closest for the best photo or quote from one of the men. As Henri later described it, "It was hell for one afternoon." In the end, they sold exclusive European rights to their story for 15 days to the *Daily Mail* for the princely sum of £7,500.

The newspaper sent a car to bring the boys to London, where they were put up in a luxury hotel and taken to chic nightclubs in Piccadilly. Each night, they laid awake in their soft beds, unable to sleep without the rocking comfort of the ocean. Moreover, they missed the kittens, their constant companions. "They cheered us up whenever we felt a little depressed," Gaston told reporters, "and, believe me, there were days of storm and high wind when we did not feel too happy."

Henri was only able to spend three days in London before he had to rush back to Canada, as Jeannine was sick. She had let him have his

FACING PAGE:
The raftsmen are feted upon their return to dry land. From left to right, are Henri, Marc and Gaston.

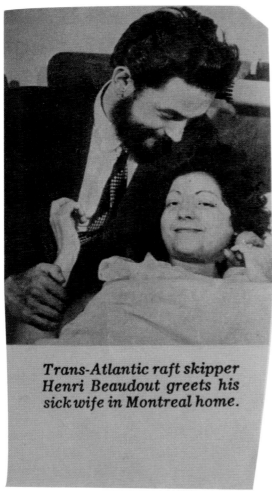

Trans-Atlantic raft skipper Henri Beaudout greets his sick wife in Montreal home.

Henri greets Jeannine upon returning home from the voyage.

FACING PAGE:
The cover of the September 1, 1956, edition of *Paris Match*.

fun, or whatever it was he'd been doing on that raft, and it was time for him to come home and resume his duties as a father and husband. On his flight back to Montreal, he politely declined his in-flight meal: fish.

For the next few weeks, *L'Égaré II* was all over the world, in black and white. It was dubbed the "Atlantic *Kon-Tiki*" by the press, a moniker that has stuck to this very day — so long is the shadow cast by Thor Heyerdahl. Nevertheless, the journey was featured in cover stories in English, French, Russian, Greek and Spanish newspapers and magazines. *Paris Match* stretched excerpts from Henri's log across two back-to-back issues. Parts of his journal were also printed in the pages of the *New York Times*. *L'Égaré II*, it seemed, was all anyone wanted to talk about.

In the various interviews and articles, the boys expressed a desire for the raft to be put in a museum. A museum in London showed interest, but officials back in Quebec convinced Henri to bring the raft home for display. As Marc put it, "it was our way of thanking that big country [Canada] for its generosity toward new immigrants like the three of us." At a cost of $3,000, the raft was shipped back to Halifax, where it was then placed on a truck and brought to Montreal.

PARIS MATCH

N° 386 SAMEDI 1er SEPTEMBRE 1956 50 Fr.

Afrique du Nord 60 fr. — Maroc 85 fr. — G. 9 4/8. — Belg. 10 fr.
Suisse 0.90 — Canada 25 cents. — Italie 15 paoli — Tunisie 65 dinar

EXCLUSIF

Le carnet de bord et
l'album de photos de

L'ÉGARÉ II

Trois hommes sur un radeau ont mis
87 jours à franchir l'Atlantique. Ils
vous racontent eux-mêmes leur extra-
ordinaire aventure en texte et en photos.
Photo René Vital.

The raftsmen meet the mayor of Montreal. Henri is seated in the middle, Jeannine is to the left of Henri and Marc is beside her. Gaston is at the far right of the frame. Mayor Jean Drapeau is to the right of Henri.

Around this time, Henri, Marc and Gaston returned to Halifax to see the people who had helped them along the way. RoseMarie got a call one day from Henri — he was in town and the CBC wanted to interview him. He had told them that he would not go on TV without his "official interpreter." When she joined him for the interview, Henri gave her a cheque and a copy of his new book, *The Lost One*, which had just been published. RoseMarie had followed the exploits of the raftsmen throughout their journey and diligently kept a scrapbook full of articles she had clipped from the local papers. As years went on, she lost touch with the men, but when she had her children, she often shared with them the story of *L'Égaré II* and the Frenchmen who made the spring of 1956 so exciting for a girl from Pointe-de-L'Église.

As for the men, the physical distance between them grew as the years passed — they couldn't have gotten much closer than they were on the raft — but by all accounts, there was never any conflict or acrimony between them during the long journey, and that continued on into their later years. They had started this journey as strangers, but they were now bonded for life.

Gaston and Henri set out to improve their fishing skills.

HENRI AND Jeannine Beaudout remained in Montreal, where they raised their daughter and still live today. In 1967, using a small sailboat called *Exocet*, Henri retraced the Atlantic voyage of Jacques Cartier. Henri would go on to form a sailing school in Rimouski, Quebec, which later moved to the Quebec Yacht Club. Like Marc, Henri embarked on several more expeditions throughout the decades, through the Pacific and the Mediterranean — however, he had the good sense to do it by sailboat, rather than by raft. But *L'Égaré II* would always hold a special place in Henri's heart — it was his first complete adventure.

THE FOOTAGE shot by Gaston Vanackere was turned into an hour-long documentary entitled *Atlantic Adventure*. The film was distributed in the U.S. by Schoenfeld Film Distributing and made its premiere in Boston on September 25, 1961. Gaston would go on to have a prominent career in tourism, until his death in 1995.

L'*ÉGARÉ II* WAS just the start of Marc Modena's high-seas adventures. Ten years after this voyage, Marc would take part in another rafting trip, this time travelling 143 days from Ecuador toward Australia aboard the balsa-wood raft *Pacifica*, with Spanish adventurer Vital Alsar. That expedition was abandoned as the balsa logs began to rot beneath their feet. However, Modena and Alsar would successfully undertake the same journey two times with *La Balsa* and *Las Balsas*. In the late 1970s, Marc graduated from rafts to Spanish galleons for two more voyages with Alsar. Marc spent a total of 572 days on the ocean on a raft. In 2005, Fréjus, France, named a quay after its favourite nautical son. Marc Modena passed away on November 15, 2011, in Dénia, Spain, at the age of 84.

LITTLE IS known of Jose Martinez' life post-*L'Égaré II*. The story that ran in the June 30, 1956, edition of *The Daily News*, out of St. John's, Newfoundland, said only of his future that he didn't think returning to his mechanic's job was going to be a possibility. He looked forward to going back home to Montreal and his wife and possibly getting into business with his father-in-law, who "makes pop," as he told *The Daily News*.

AND THE KITTENS ... Puce and Guiton didn't return to Canada with the rest of the crew. They spent six months in quarantine, after which they were adopted by the Duke and Duchess of Bedford. The two kittens lived out the remainder of their days on the 1,200-hectare (3,000-acre) estate of Woburn Abbey. The duke and duchess even moored a model of the raft in their lake as a permanent home for the kittens.

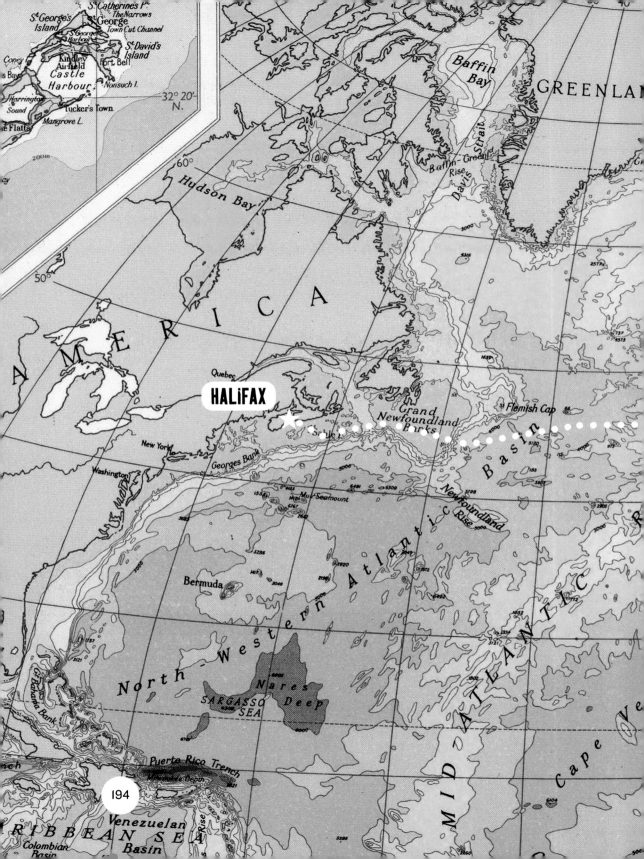

St George's
Island
St Catherine's Pt
The Narrows
George
Town Cut Channel
St David's
Island
Fort Bell
Coney
Kindley
Airfield
Castle
Harbour
Nonsuch I.
Harrington
Sound
Tucker's Town
Mangrove L.
e Flatts
200m
32° 20'
N.

Baffin
Bay
GREENLAN

60°
Hudson Bay
Baffin-Greenl
Davis
Strait
Rise

50°

A M E R I C A

Quebec

HALiFAX

Grand
Newfoundland
Banks
St Flemish Cap

New York
Sable I.

Washington
Georges Bank

Newfoundland
Rise

Basin

Bermuda

Mur Seamount

N o r t h - W e s t e r n   A t l a n t i c

A t l a n t i c

Nares
Deep

SARGASSO
SEA

M I D - A T L A N T I C

Cape Ve

194

Puerto Rico Trench

Venezuelan

RIBBEAN SEA
Basin
Colombian
Basin

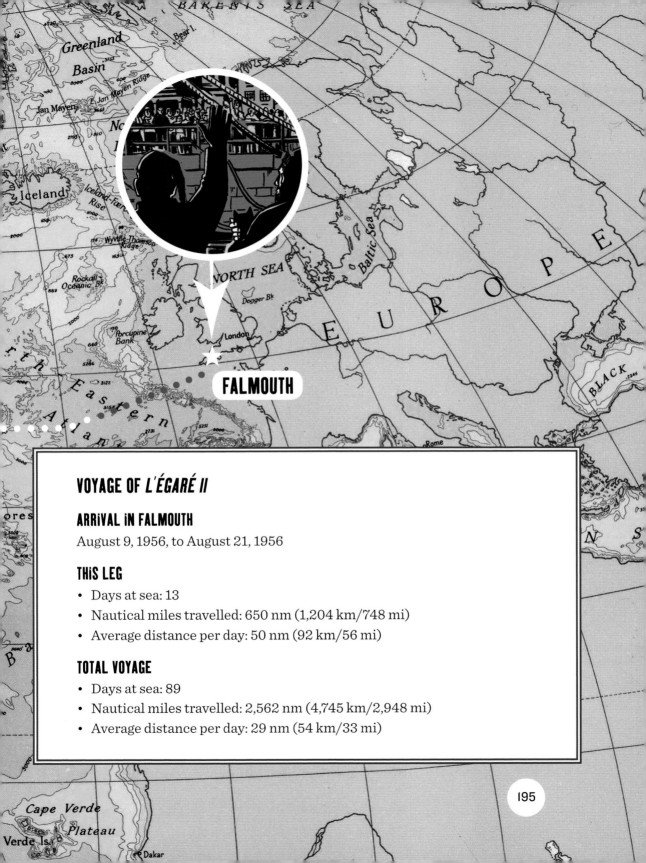

VOYAGE OF *L'ÉGARÉ II*

ARRIVAL IN FALMOUTH

August 9, 1956, to August 21, 1956

THIS LEG

- Days at sea: 13
- Nautical miles travelled: 650 nm (1,204 km/748 mi)
- Average distance per day: 50 nm (92 km/56 mi)

TOTAL VOYAGE

- Days at sea: 89
- Nautical miles travelled: 2,562 nm (4,745 km/2,948 mi)
- Average distance per day: 29 nm (54 km/33 mi)

FALMOUTH

EPiLOGUE

"IT WAS NOT the grand gesture the late Quebec premier Maurice Duplessis promised 60 years ago, but it should reassure 89-year-old Henri Beaudout that the memory of his remarkable voyage across the Atlantic will not die with him."
– *Montreal Gazette*, July 14, 2016

ON A CRISP March evening in 2012, Louis Hardy met Henri Beaudout face to face for the very first time. Beaudout was sick as a dog, gripped by a terrible cold.

"It was my wife who gave me this," he told Louis. "She was sick all last week and I got it from her."

Henri was 84 years old — just about to turn 85 — and to Louis, he appeared quite feeble. Beaudout had driven himself the three hours from Montreal to Quebec City to deliver a symposium on the journey of *L'Égaré II* as part of the Salon du Bateau de Québec. Attendance was poor that night, just a handful of walk-ins supplemented by the friends and family that Hardy could persuade to attend — a concerted effort on his part to put bums in seats, as it was he who was responsible for bringing Henri Beaudout to the conference.

When *L'Égaré II* arrived in Falmouth, England, in August 1956, it made international headlines — the "crazy Frenchmen" were splashed across the cover of *Paris Match* and in the pages of *Le Figaro* and others. But in the intervening half-century, their story had slipped out of the collective consciousness. Indeed, even those who had been involved in preparing

Radar was one of the many French-language magazines to run the story of *L'Égaré II.*

La mer est démontée. Des lames de 20 mètres de creux. La tempête sévit depuis un mois. En plein Atlantique, trois hommes épuisés, émules des héros du "Kon-Tiki", hissent le lugubre drapeau noir du désastre...

for the trip would only passingly wonder, "Whatever happened to that raft and its crew?"

Louis Hardy had his own connection to the raft: he had grown up with it. Born in 1950, Hardy was just five years old when the first *L'Égaré* drifted past his hometown of Neuville, Quebec. A little village located on the north shore of the St. Lawrence River, Neuville had very few things — it didn't have a hospital or any fire service — but it did have a train station, useful for transporting the abundant corn crops that were a staple of the community. It also had a church, Saint-François-de-Sales, named for the patron saint of writers and journalists, which dated back to the 17th century. And, as it turns out, Neuville also had the good ship *L'Égaré II* for a time. How it ended up there was by a rather tortuous set of circumstances.

Henri, left, Gaston, middle, and Marc in London following the conclusion of their 89-day voyage.

As the crew of *L'Égaré II* was feted in England, a representative from the National Maritime Museum in London approached Henri about putting the raft on exhibition. At some point soon after, Henri was on a phone call with a minister from the Quebec National Assembly. When Henri told him what he was considering doing with the vessel, the minister was quick to respond: "Don't leave your raft with the English," he told him. "It belongs in Quebec. Bring it back here and we'll put it in a museum."

Henri, left, and Marc, right, take the canvas cover off the cabin of *L'Égaré II* to expose the hand-woven laths of wood underneath.

And so Henri paid to ship his 10-ton raft back to Canada. The three raftsmen took their vessel to the Montreal Sportsmen Show in 1957, but no further plans were made. At the time, there were no institutions, Quebecois or otherwise, that could or would take on a 9-metre (30-foot) raft, something the minister had failed to mention. For the time being, Henri thought, he would store *L'Égaré II* temporarily at the Motel L'Égaré located off highway 138, which ran right through Neuville.

The motel was not named for the raft, but rather, its proprietor, the auspiciously named Monsieur L'Égaré. Mr. L'Égaré saw an opportunity to provide a home for "the lost one." The raft would serve as a roadside attraction for vacationers passing his motel and campground — a point of interest that might entice them to stop in, maybe stay the night.

Louis Hardy remembers the raft fondly. It was an object of fascination for all the boys and girls who crossed its path on their way to the public pool located on L'Égaré's campground. They didn't get *Paris Match* or *Le Figaro* in Neuville, and by the time the raft landed in the village, the story was already a few years old, long out of the news cycle. The kids of Neuville had to go on rumours and half-remembered accounts from their parents to piece together the story of *L'Égaré II*.

Road sign for the L'Égaré campgound in Neuville, Quebec.

As Hardy would remember years later, it was the dark years of the Maurice Duplessis government in Quebec, and there was little Quebecers took pride in: "Maurice Richard, and maybe [professional wrestler] Johnny Rougeau, but that's about it." For Hardy, then and now, the raftsmen are French-Canadian folk heroes. They could stand shoulder to shoulder with logger Big Joe Mufferaw or strongman Louis Cyr. But that's not how things went. The raft remained on the side of route 138 for the better part of a decade. Unprotected from the elements, it slowly fell into disrepair. Eventually, it was scavenged for wood by a local shop owner looking to demarcate the property line between his home and his business. This potential icon of Quebec folklore was reduced to a fence.

In the summer of 2011, Hardy was recently retired from Radio-Canada in Montreal, the French-language service of the Canadian Broadcasting Corporation. The boy who grew up in the twin shadows of *L'Égaré II*'s mast and the spires of Saint-François-de-Sales had picked the only career that made sense to him: sports reporter. In his 30-year career with Radio-Canada, he had covered everything from the Olympic Games to the exploits of Quebecois adventurer Bernard Voyer. One afternoon, while browsing through the Librairie Raffin in Place Versailles shopping centre, Hardy spotted the familiar silhouette of *L'Égaré II* on a book cover. He had stumbled upon *Les égarés*, a new edition of the 1957 account of the journey, updated and self-published by Beaudout. Reading the book was Hardy's first opportunity to learn the whole incredible story of the 89-day transatlantic adventure.

With a renewed interest, and armed with further details (like the raftsmen's names, for instance), Hardy began researching the story. He located a copy of *Le Figaro* from August 1956 that carried a feature on Beaudout and his crew. Hardy then approached his friend Michel Sacco with the book and the article. As editor-in-chief of the French-language sailing magazine *L'escale nautique*, perhaps Sacco could locate Henri Beaudout, Hardy thought. His instincts proved wise, as it only took his friend a couple of weeks to find a phone number. Henri was still around, not living in France, as Hardy feared, but nearby in the Montreal suburb of Anjou, not a three-minute drive from where he had found the book.

After delivering his symposium that evening in March 2012, Henri Beaudout asked Hardy to drive him back to the Hotel Belley on Saint Paul Street. When they arrived, Louis had to help the ailing Henri up the flight of stairs to his room. Beaudout then asked him if he could fetch something to combat his hypoglycemia. Louis ran across the street to the nearest depanneur and bought two Mars bars. When Louis returned to the hotel, Henri was shivering under the blankets in his bed. Dropping off the chocolate, he left the former skipper in his hotel room to sleep off his cold. The next day, Hardy called the hotel only to find that Beaudout had already checked out. He then called his home and Jeannine confirmed that Henri was currently driving himself back to Montreal. What Louis didn't know then was that he had taken the first steps down a path with Henri Beaudout that would go on for years and end in no less than the re-creation of the raft he so admired as a boy.

Henri Beaudout's appearance at the 2012 Salon du Bateau de Québec was the start of a new chapter. At 85, life had picked up momentum. Henri was hardly the feeble old man whom Hardy had first met; he had vigour and telling his story to new audiences enlivened him. He spent his time touring around Quebec preaching the gospel of a *L'Égaré II* rebuild. Newspapers and magazines were once again printing the name *L'Égaré II*, though not on the scale they had before. The first, a six-page feature written by Sacco, appeared in the fall issue of *L'escale nautique*. This was followed by several pieces by the CBC Newfoundland reporter Marie Wadden.

Wadden was my introduction to Henri Beaudout. If you read my introduction to this book, you'll remember that I drove seven and a half hours from Toronto to see Henri speak in Neuville, Quebec. My goal was to introduce myself and convince Henri to participate in making a documentary with me. Truth is, I became self-conscious about my French and never did introduce myself. After hearing the piece on *L'Égaré II* that Wadden did for the CBC radio program *C'est la vie*, I immediately contacted her. She could not have been kinder, convincing me my French was adequate and encouraging me to get in touch with Henri. That bit of encouragement led me down a path that I would follow for the next four years.

My first meeting with Henri Beaudout was in October of 2012, at his condo in Anjou, where he still lives with Jeannine and a small, fluffy dog. I had gone there with an image in my head of what his home would look like — I imagined maps, taxidermy and any number of sailing paraphernalia on display. He had been a pilot and a mariner and was a hunter and consummate fly fisherman. I was expecting a home worthy of Papa Hemingway. However, much to my surprise, my home is closer to Hemingway's than Henri's is. His place is shockingly pastel in its palette, with white wall-to-wall carpeting and porcelain tchotchkes everywhere. The condo is all Mrs. Beaudout — no trace of Henri's past is on display. That afternoon, he served me coffee and cookies and asked me questions like, "What does your father do for a living?" (When I told him he was a purchasing agent for a mining company, Henri seemed disappointed — nothing in common there, I suppose.)

I then launched into it: "M. Beaudout," I said in my best French, "I want to help you and rebuild your raft, and I want to make a documentary film on you and the process."

His exact reply escapes me, but I don't remember having to convince him of anything. By the end of our conversation, he said: "We have a saying in French: now we're shipmates." I told him there was a similar expression in English. It was in that moment that I understood how Henri Beaudout had convinced those other men to put their lives in his hands and cross the Atlantic on a raft of his own design. As Louis once said to me, "If Henri Beaudout puts his confidence in you, you'll do anything not to let him down."

This was the plan: to find a museum that was willing to rebuild and permanently house a reconstructed *L'Égaré II*. I was enlisted as the designated cameraman of this new adventure. Louis was the first mate, cold-calling institutions to see if they were in desperate need of a 9-metre (30-foot) raft. Marie Wadden continued her media blitz, publishing articles and producing radio pieces. Joining this new team was the original fifth Beatle, RoseMarie Comeau (now Maher) heading up East Coast operations. The former site of the Dartmouth Slip had become a condo development. RoseMarie was working to see whether she could get a plaque dedicated to *L'Égaré II* into the development, somehow.

Henri, Jeannine and a friend pose with an airplane in the early 1950s.

For my part, I launched an Indiegogo campaign, and because I had created a website to support it, members of the public started contacting me about the raft. The most interesting inquiry was from a gentleman in Scotland named Michael Dutton who owned a business building log cabins. At the time, he was planning his own rafting trip across the Atlantic. "Dear Ryan," he started.

I am starting to build a raft as of next week to raise money through sponsorship for the charity BuildAid. I was intending to build the raft from machine-rounded logs, which would be a more modern version of what Henri built, although I could always change my plans at this early stage. I don't have a timeline as of yet, as I am still planning the venture. Although, as a training exercise, I was intending to sail the raft on Loch Ness, once up the Loch and once down, and I have a crew for this; however, finding someone as mad as myself willing to sail the Atlantic on the raft is a slightly different matter and challenge.

Henri was scheduled to present at the 2013 edition of the Salon du Bateau for two nights in February. I went along to film, and once again, it was spotty attendance. But as I had come to observe, what Henri's audiences lacked in numbers, they made up for in enthusiasm. I was vibrating with the exciting news that we could possibly have someone to build our raft, and he was willing to do it for nothing. I figured we had solved 50 per cent of our problems. However, when I told Henri, he saw it differently.

The first thing he did was tear apart Dutton's plan to sail from Scotland to Canada. "That's not how the ocean currents work," he lectured me. "If he leaves from Scotland, he will end up in the Caribbean" — a point on which Henri was totally correct, in fact. In 2015, at the age of 84, British broadcaster and adventurer Anthony

Smith did a similar trip, sailing the Atlantic by raft, starting from the Canary Islands and eventually landing on the Bahamian island of Eleuthera. That was one reason why Dutton's proposal was not attractive to him, but what became apparent to me only then was that Beaudout wanted to be involved in the rebuilding. He, Henri Beaudout, wanted to rebuild his beloved raft. So it was a no to the Scot.

Henri Beaudout was staring out the window of a train. Recording him on her iPhone, Marie Wadden asked, "Where are you going, Henri Beaudout?"

"Comment?"

"Where are you going?" she asked once more, holding the microphone closer to his mouth. He leaned in.

"To New York," he answered and turned back to the window.

"To do what?"

"My favourite journalist is going to receive an international award of excellence."

It was June 22, 2014. The journalist and her subject were travelling together by Amtrak from Montreal to New York for the New York Festivals 2014 International Radio Program Awards. Wadden was due to receive the Silver Radio award for her audio documentary *The Atlantic Kon-Tiki*, a piece that had aired the previous October as part of the CBC Radio program *Living Out Loud*. Beaudout was very happy for Wadden, who, by this point, had become a friend. In accepting her award, Marie Wadden brought him on stage with her. He then addressed the crowd in French: "I want to thank Marie, without whom I would not be here tonight to tell you that I'm continuing to fight to achieve *my dream*." He emphasized the last two words in English.

Progress had stalled on the rebuilding of *L'Égaré II*: Michael Dutton's planned raft was a wash and the crowdfunding campaign had fizzled. Henri had more speaking dates, including one in St-Pierre

and Miquelon, but these just passed the time and never amounted to concrete progress.

Marie Wadden had contacted the Maritime Museum of the Atlantic to see if she might get them on board for an exhibition. It seemed a natural fit that the raft would go into this Halifax institution, the oldest and largest maritime museum in the country. However, the museum administration showed only a tacit interest in creating a maquette for display. For Beaudout, however, this didn't constitute the dream — a model would not suffice, and so he would have to wait and continue working.

It was not such a far-fetched dream — Oslo, Sweden, has an entire museum dedicated to the *Kon-Tiki*. In Australia, the Ballina Naval and Maritime Museum houses one of the three rafts that traversed the Pacific as part of *Las Balsas,* an oceanic adventure embarked on by Marc Modena. If *Kon-Tiki* had its own museum and one of Marc's other rafts was likewise venerated, then surely *L'Égaré II* — the Atlantic *Kon-Tiki,* as Beaudout would be loathe to say — merited some sort of similar recognition.

Then, in September 2014, the rebuild project hit its own Gulf Stream. Yves Paquette, the director general of the Maritime Association of Quebec, pledged $10,000 toward a *L'Égaré II* exhibit. Moreover, there was renewed interest from the Musée maritime du Québec (MMQ), which had earlier dismissed the project. A change in management, coupled with the fact that board president Simon-Pierre Paré had grown up not far from Neuville and had childhood memories of *L'Égaré II*, opened new doors for the possible exhibit.

As Louis Hardy was working with the institutions, Henri sought vendors to mitigate the costs of the project. He was raft building all over again, wheeling and dealing, sourcing the necessary materials — he managed to get a sailmaker to donate his time and materials to the project. This was October of 2014.

Finally, in July 2016, a *L'Égaré II* exhibit opened at the Musée maritime du Québec in L'Islet, a village not unlike Neuville. It too has no hospital or professional fire service for its 4,000 residents, but it does have the Notre-Dame-de-Bonsecours, a church dating back to 1768.

It is also the birthplace of the Canadian Arctic explorer Captain Joseph-Elzéar Bernier. Around the turn of the 20th century, Bernier piloted his steamship *Arctic* through the northern waters on annual trips to collect duties from whalers and traders operating in the area. During these trips, he and his crew would explore the uninhabited islands, unearthing caches left by earlier explorers. In July 1909, he erected a plaque on Melville Island, the spot where 19th-century explorer Sir William Parry had spent 10 months frozen in, some 100 years earlier. With this plaque, Bernier officially claimed the Arctic Archipelago in the name of Canada.

In 1968, the Marine Association of the Saint Lawrence Valley established one of the first institutions dedicated to the conservation of historical ships. Its full name — Musée maritime du Québec: Capitaine

A faithful I:3 scale recreation of the raft, cats included, in the L'Atlantique en radeau exhibit in the Musée maritime du Québec.

J. E. Bernier — honours L'Islet's favourite son. This museum had long been involved in conversations about partnering to re-create *L'Égaré II*, but progress had been slow. Residents of L'Islet would have certainly seen *L'Égaré I* drift past their homes on the south shore of the St. Lawrence River back in 1955.

Located in a former convent, the MMQ is unusual in that it has actual ships on permanent display: the sailboat *J. E. Bernier II*, the hydrofoil HMCS *Bras d'Or 400* and the icebreaker CCGS *Ernest LaPointe* all stand grounded on the back lawn as "ship museums," open for touring by the public. It was initially considered that *L'Égaré II 2.0* could join this collection as an interactive exhibit that kids could climb on and explore. However, as the project was further scrutinized, it was deemed too unsafe, and to add the hardware required for safety would compromise the historical accuracy of the exhibit. Eventually, the plan for building a full-scale raft was

The exhibit features profiles of the raftsmen, as well as graphics on sea conditions, the marine life they saw and much more.

scuttled. If the museum were to do the exhibit, Henri would have to compromise on his dream.

The result was a 1:3 scale recreation of *L'Égaré II*, built by cabinet-maker Gaston Chouinard. Perhaps a 3-metre (10-foot) replica didn't fulfill Henri's "final dream," as he had once called it in a radio interview, nor was it the grand gesture the Quebec minister had promised 60 years ago, but as Marie Wadden noted in the *Montreal Gazette*, "it should reassure 89-year-old Henri Beaudout that the memory of his remarkable voyage across the Atlantic will not die with him."

And so, on the 60th anniversary of the expedition, the MMQ, an established Quebec institution, launched the exhibit on *L'Égaré II*. There to mark the occasion with Henri was Louis Hardy, Marie Wadden, Yves Paquette and many other friends Henri had made in the pursuit of this dream. I was there, too. My documentary *The Raftsmen* is part of the exhibit.

A view of the starboard side of the 1:3 scale raft, showing the partly covered cabin of woven laths.

L'Islet-sur-Mer, Quebec, 2016

This museum is beautiful.

Oh Papa! There it is ...

It took Monsieur Chouinard 300 hours to construct it.

Monsieur Beaudout ...

... how does it feel to see your raft once more?

I first dreamed of L'Égaré at a time in my life when dreams meant very little.

I had seen humanity at its worst, and it traumatized me ...

... for years.

It was the voyage of L'Égaré II that freed me.

I'll never forget that.

On July 15, 2016, the day the exhibit was due to open, Henri and I sat together, not to film — that part of our journey together was done — but to eat lunch. He had come with his daughter, and I was with my wife and our five-month-old girl. My obsession with Henri's 88 days at sea had occupied four years of my life. In the end, I realized that the size of the replica was not so important; it would never be *L'Égaré II*. Henri's raft was gone. When I met Henri Beaudout, I was a graduate student, and now here we sat together in L'Islet all those years later as husbands and fathers. The time for grand gestures was done. Henri's name is engraved in the historical record through the museum, the documentary and this very book, but his true legacy is his co-conspirators, among which I count myself.

ACKNOWLEDGEMENTS

THIS BOOK would not have been possible without the support and contributions of many people along the way. I wish to express my sincerest gratitude to all those who helped me in ways big and small, and my indebtedness in particular to the following:

The Beaudouts: Henri, for the countless hours you have given to me throughout the years and for a friendship that I will cherish for a lifetime. Jeannine and Chantal, thank you for sharing your husband and father with me and for your family's story.

Marie Wadden, who shared everything with me and without whom I would not have had the opportunity to do this book.

Louis Hardy for your continual support and enthusiasm for all things *L'Égaré*.

RoseMarie Comeau-Maher for inviting us into your home, connecting us with other characters in this story and sharing your memories and photographs.

Mireille Modena for spiriting the rarest of memoirs, your father's book, my way late into the research process for this book.

Joan Fluelling, Remi Morissette and the late Captain Cyril Henneberry for sitting down with me so many years ago.

Steve Cameron and Dmitry Bondarenko for being stellar partners in this endeavour.

Marijke Friesen, Catherine Dorton, Jessie Durham, as well as the staff at Firefly Books, for their help and expertise.

Luca Caminati for green-lighting the initial major research project that lead me here.

And finally, to Jose, Marc and Gaston.

— Ryan Barnett

FURTHER READING

"87 jours sur un radeau," *Paris Match*, September 8, 1956, 52–61.

Atlantic Adventure, directed by Gaston Vanackere and Henri Beaudout. Canada: Schoenfeld Film Distributing, 1961.

Beaudout, Henri. *Les Égarés*. Raleigh: Lulu.com, 2007.

Beaudout, Henri. *Les Tribulations de Bob Brumas*. Belœil, Quebec: Les Éditions la Caboche, 2009.

Beaudout, Henri. *The Lost One*. Suffolk: Hodder & Stoughton Limited, 1957.

"L'Aventure de *L'Égaré II*," *Paris Match*, September 1, 1956, 46–58.

Modena, Marc, and Marc Moity. *L'argonaute*. Valencia : Imprenta Rapida Llorens, S.L., 2000.

The Raftsmen, directed by Ryan Barnett. Toronto: 2016.

Wadden, Marie. *Atlantic Kon-Tiki*, from Living Out Loud. Toronto: CBC Radio, 2014.

A NOTE ON THE PHOTOGRAPHS

L' *ÉGARÉ II* IS a special story for many reasons, but one of the things that makes the tale of the voyage so appealing is that the crew left behind a visual record.

Gaston Vanackere made sure he took both still photography and film footage of the 89-day expedition; he is the author of the majority of the pictures in this book. Gaston's record provides a glimpse into life on the raft that is difficult to capture in words. Take, for instance, the image on page 112, which shows Marc and Henri tied to the interior of the cabin, waiting out a storm. The pair look tired and defeated. It isn't hard to imagine how hopeless they felt, stuck there — sometimes for days at a time — as a storm raged. This image is one of the few that reveals this side of the adventure, as Gaston, too, was part of all the happenings on the raft. For him, capturing images sometimes took a back seat to staying alive.

Another remarkable set of images illustrating a difficult to articulate concept are those of the *General R.E. Callan* (pages 141 & 143). That the 9-metre (30-foot), 10-ton *L'Égaré II* shared the water with many ships like the 10,000-ton Navy transport is easily forgotten. The incredible size difference and the danger to the men on the raft are equally hard to qualify without pictures. Gaston's photos provide a view as to the scale of this constant danger to the expedition.

This book owes a lot to Gaston's work. His record captured all manner of life aboard the raft, and it is with great pride and admiration that it is included here.

— Steve Cameron, editor

ARTIST'S SKETCHBOOK

Artist's sketch of a comic, originally planned for "Sick Man Aboard," that was cut for pacing. The intent was to show the various roles the kittens served on the raft, from shipmates to barometers to confidantes.

The artist's sketch and inks of a portion of "The Rescue," which appears in "The Story of *L'Égaré I.*"

Character studies of *L'Égaré II* and the
three raftsmen who made the voyage to
England. Henri is sketched holding the
fish, Gaston with the camera and Marc
with the radio.